EMPOWERED

The Secret to Armanino's Success

BY ANDREW J. ARMANINO, III MATTHEW J. ARMANINO MARY E. TRESSEL

Dedication:

In honor and gratitude to the original entrepreneurs:
Andy Armanino and Tom Jones

All proceeds from the sale of this book will support the grantmaking and community service efforts of the Armanino Foundation.

www.armaninofoundation.org

Table of

Contents

01.

Building the Foundation | PG. 1

02.

Never Satisfied | PG. 27

03.

Striking a Balance | PG. 56

04.

Our Finest Moment | **PG. 91**

05.

Giving Our People a Voice | **PG. 141**

06.

Our Best Days Are Ahead | **PG. 151**

Foreward

Sometimes there is something amazing in your own backyard that you take for granted, and then one day you learn how special it is and you wonder how you could have gone so long without realizing it. I grew up within a relatively short drive of Yosemite, and never went there until I was an adult. How could that be?

Well, in the context of the world of financial services firms, Armanino is like Yosemite. It has been a local gem that I never completely appreciated until I stepped back and considered it in the larger context of organizational success.

Ironically, I knew of the firm quite well for years, both because my own firm was a client, and the local church I go to used their services. Heck, I even worked with Andy Armanino and his executive team! It's not that I didn't appreciate the quality of the firm's work. Not at all. It's just that I didn't quite realize how successful they were, how they came to be such a cutting-edge firm, and how many other people benefitted from their work.

This book puts all of that into perspective and will be interesting and helpful for a variety of different audiences. For those who have worked with Armanino, it will put the pieces of the puzzle together and provide the whole picture. For those considering working with the firm, it will provide the best possible insights for evaluating your decision (I think I know what you'll decide). But most important of all, for anyone building a services firm, it will offer a real-world case study on how to combine innovation, entrepreneurial dexterity, customer service and employee morale.

Whoever you are and no matter what your reasons for taking a look at the book in your hands, I think you'll find more than a few interesting insights here, as well as some practical guidance that can change the way your organization operates.

Patrick Lencioni,
New York Times Best-Selling Author and President, The Table Group

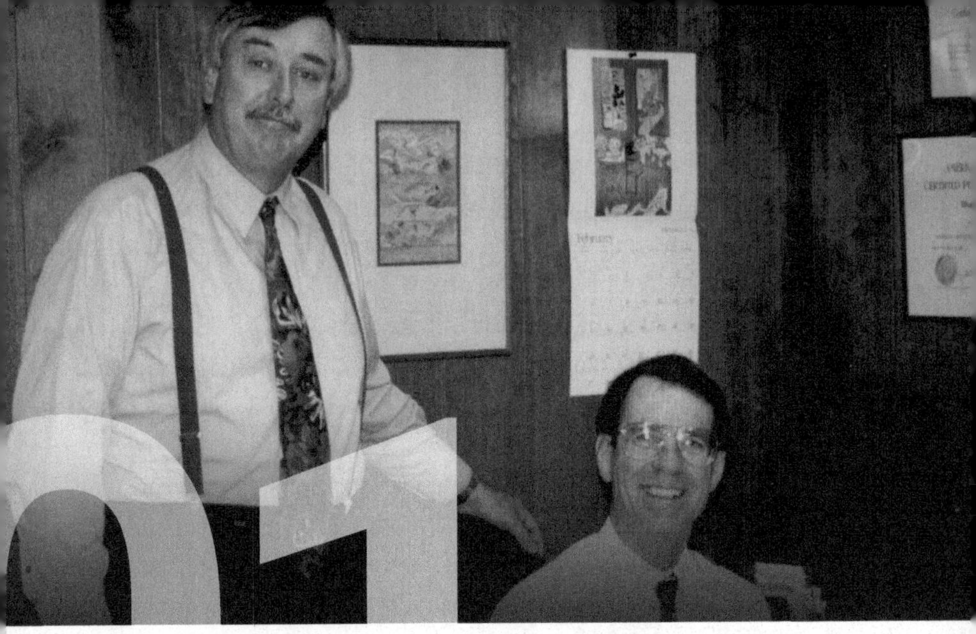

Building the Foundation

1969-2004 | By Andy Armanino

> Armanino is the most unique accounting firm I've ever seen. It exemplifies the reason we should preserve firms with their own identity.
>
> - Anton Colella, Chief Executive Officer, Moore Global

On a chilly, late winter day in 1969, my dad, Andy Armanino, and Tom Jones stood looking out the window of their tiny office on East 14th in San Leandro, California. When they saw the mailman going down the other side of the street, both men hurried back to their respective desks, picked up their pencils and furiously committed themselves to their client work papers. With no thought to the impact of his everyday task, the mailman dropped an envelope in the slot labeled "Armanino & Jones, Accountants" and walked away.

As his steps receded, my dad and Tom ran to the door. A former Whitworth College quarterback, Tom won the footrace, reached into the mail slot, and tore open the envelope. "A check!" he cheered, and they both laughed with relief. They would celebrate together that evening with a beer and the satisfaction that they could pay the bills and feed their growing families for another month.

These were the humble beginnings of today's Armanino, the 21st largest firm in the United States with more than 2,000 professionals and 20 offices across the nation. Our firm's unparalleled growth over the last 52 years catapulted us from anonymity to a temporary reputation as the "Bad Boys and Girls of Accounting" to our current stature as one of the most respected, award-winning, innovative firms in the nation.

THE ORIGINAL ENTREPRENEURS

Armanino's founders launched their accounting careers together as staff auditors at Coopers & Lybrand when my dad and Tom were sent to the Midwest for a six-week training program. They were the only two staff members at the small Oakland outpost of the Big 8 firm and they made an immediate and lifelong friendship. Over the next four and a half years, they were promoted to supervisors, guiding the work of younger staffers, and observing the inner workings of the international firm. Dad and Tom also spent a lot of time together outside of the office, along with their wives, living just three blocks apart in Alameda. The foursome all enjoyed one another's company, and the wives often took their kids for walks and playdates together.

Tom and Dad worked on different engagements, getting comfortable helping business owners with more than audit, bookkeeping and tax engagements. Their clients started to call them directly, instead of the Coopers partner on the account, seeking advice on growing their businesses or whether they should move forward with an acquisition. The two soon realized they found greater fulfillment working directly with clients, rather than being supervisors.

"We wanted to be our own bosses," said Tom. "We really liked working with the clients, getting our hands dirty."

The leap from "There's got to be a better way" to launching their own firm occurred when one of Tom's clients said he'd give him as much work as he could handle on his own at $10/hour. This was the break Tom and my dad had been waiting for.

"When we turned in our resignations, we were surprised and pleased that the Coopers partners told us how wonderful we were," my dad told me. "We hadn't heard that very often in the four and a half years we'd worked there."

To ensure that none of his clients were left unattended, Dad agreed to continue servicing his accounts on a per diem basis for Coopers. With the promise of Medicare audits from Tom's client Blue Cross and Dad's contract work, the pair felt confident that success was theirs for the taking. On February 1, 1969, Armanino & Jones, Accountants was launched.

"Andy and I really trusted each other and knew we could rely on each other," said Tom.

He learned just days later that Blue Cross now considered the new firm too small and would not send any of the promised Medicare audit work their way. Undaunted, Dad deposited his per diem checks from Coopers in the partnership account and the fledgling firm survived the first few months on contract work. Thus, the celebration ritual began when a check arrived by mail.

"There was never a time I thought this wasn't going to work," Dad said. "We would out-hustle and out-work everyone else to grow our business."

Dad and Tom soon became familiar faces in the industrial city of San Leandro. Public Accountant Joe DeSchmidt had been practicing in the city for many years and was nearing retirement when Armanino & Jones opened their doors. Just six months later, he met with the two young men and offered to sell off his bookkeeping accounts on a retained gross basis while he kept his tax clients.

"It turned out that Joe had wonderful clients in construction, manufacturing, bars and restaurants," said Tom. "We earned a set fee for each client, and our wives, Kathy and Monica, would type the financial statements for us."

The firm soon flourished with these bookkeeping clients, individual tax returns and large audits for World Airways and Insurance Securities in San Francisco. Adding one bookkeeper and then another to manage the day-to-day work, Dad and Tom spent more time in their clients' offices, answering their business concerns.

"We wanted to wrap our arms around our clients, really get to know them and help them achieve their dreams," Dad said.

This in-depth focus on client needs helped establish a reputation for Armanino & Jones as a solid, honest, hardworking firm and the practice grew. When they added more staff, Tom and Dad turned their negative Big 8 experiences, like the lack of feedback on their own performance and the long wait for advancement at Coopers, into guideposts for how they would treat their own team.

"Our only exposure to other firms was Coopers. I saw an environment at Coopers that was selective, and we didn't want to be like that," said Dad. "We hired an IRS agent who was great at his job. He was also a hippie who didn't wear shoes, but that didn't matter to us.

"We helped create an atmosphere of honesty between partners and staff. We wanted everyone to feel like the firm had their backs. We wanted them to know that we appreciated them. We'd take people with us to our clients and give the staff opportunities to learn a variety of things," he said.

In 1973, Chris Frederiksen, CPA, approached Dad and Tom. With offices in San Leandro and San Francisco and a plan to provide business development consulting to other accounting firms, Chris was ready to divest of his San Leandro client base. Another acquisition was completed, and Armanino & Jones celebrated its success with as much enthusiasm as they had celebrated the firm's first checks that arrived by mail.

"When we added more staff and clients, our office parties would be spontaneous: a bag of potato chips, some snacks and beer," said Dad. "We'd all sit on the floor and talk and laugh. As a small firm, we were a family."

THE GARBAGE GUYS

The next knock on the firm's door was from Dick Lombardi in 1976. A tax partner at Kimbell, McKenna & von Kaschnitz, he told Tom and Dad that he had an opportunity to leave his firm and purchase Ed Ageno's accounting practice. Dick was confident he could handle the tax accounts, but he didn't have audit and bookkeeping experience for the rest of the business. Relying on the formula that has remained a staple of the firm's success for more than 50 years, Armanino & Jones saw how this merger could provide great opportunities for their team and moved forward quickly with the deal.

"Ed Ageno's practice was a jewel," said Dad. "He had a lot of good clients, and I took on Oakland Scavenger in 1977. This was our introduction into the solid waste business, and we learned a lot from these clients because they were people who took pride in what they did. "

Oakland Scavenger was bigger than our firm and Dad was hitting above his league at the time. It became a hallmark client for Armanino, Jones & Lombardi, proof that they could help a client achieve their goals and ambitions on a larger scale. In addition to standard tax and audit services, the engagement was consultative in nature and my dad soon became the CEO's advisor on all business matters. For instance, the firm helped Oakland Scavenger form a conglomerate with Richmond Disposal, Golden Gate Disposal, and Sunset Disposal to acquire a container company as a cost-savings move. My dad had a fundamental belief that business owners needed and wanted help making decisions. He'd often say, "It almost doesn't matter whether you are right or wrong with your advice. Helping clients move forward is what matters. If your advice is right, great. If not, you can adjust. The client will remember that you helped them with their burden."

With the solid waste practice now a big part of the firm's revenue, Armanino, Jones & Lombardi was invited to interview with the owner of Turk Island Disposal and San Leandro Landfill. Dad and Tom hired Joe Moore as a temporary accountant to attend the interview and help win the business. Not your average accounting undergrad, Joe entered the profession in a unique way.

"I was a chauffeur for a businessman who sold real estate tax shelters to doctors in the 70s," said Joe. "I worked for him for my first three years of college, driving him from Northern California through the Valley to Los Angeles. In between drives, I would do a little bookkeeping for him and that's when I decided to switch majors from math to accounting.

"When Andy and Tom reached out to me, I had graduated from Cal State Hayward with my accounting degree and was digging ditches in San Ramon not far from the firm's current headquarters," said Joe. "I threw my shovel in the trunk to take a 50 percent pay cut and joined the firm on Valentine's Day, February 14, 1977. It's been a love affair ever since."

Joe's temporary position became permanent, and he was a constant fixture at Oakland Scavenger, spending his first six months at the client site. He became our firm's solid waste subject matter expert and worked at Valley Disposal, Brentwood Disposal, Waste Management and Redwood Disposal. Much like my dad gained valuable staff management insights from his work with the firm's solid waste clients, Joe picked up some valuable business development expertise in the field.

"Every day we were out of the office and at the client site, we almost always got another project," said Joe. "We built relationships with our clients, helped them build their businesses and recognized what they needed in order to be successful."

The projects the firm undertook for their solid waste clients ranged from bookkeeping, tax, and audit to more complex business consulting engagements that included merger and acquisition activities, modeling, regulatory compliance, rate application processes and more. Dad, Tom, Dick, Joe, Paul Bottini, and the rest of the firm built such a solid reputation in the solid waste industry that they became known as "The Garbage Guys" throughout Northern California.

EARLY EXPANSION

Nancy Koo then joined the firm straight out of college when it was just fourteen people strong. She took immediately to the work ethic and was assigned to support the firm's construction clients.

"I made mistakes, that's how I learned," said Nancy. "One time, I made the same mistake two years in a row for Paul's client. When I apologized to Paul, I learned a valuable lesson because he replied, 'It's easy for you to say. I'm the one who has to face the client.'

"So, I told myself, 'I need to become a partner to face the client myself.'"

After a brief departure to give the Big 8 a try, Nancy returned at my dad's request and became the first female partner at Armanino, Jones & Lombardi.

As the firm kept expanding, our founders knew they needed a professional back-office team to continue their exemplary client service. Seventeen-year-old Cathy Harrington had just graduated from high school and following her parents' guidance to "get a job," she interviewed at the firm.

"Cathy was the fastest, most accurate typist we'd ever seen, and Tom hired her on the spot," said my dad. "A few years later, she married, had her son Richard, and was commuting from her new home in Modesto to San Leandro. She got a job offer closer to home, but I couldn't let her go. So, I topped the salary they offered, and she's been the firm's most loyal employee ever since."

As Cathy tells the story, "I was pretty much a kid myself when I started. We had good bread-and-butter clients. I never knew what they were doing out in the field. I just knew when we got a new client, I would get more work to do. I thought, 'If we could get a couple more clients, we'd really be something.'

"If somebody had a win, it was a big win for all of us and it was worth celebrating. I wasn't even old enough to drink and couldn't buy the beer, but we all gathered around the reception counter and had a great time," said Cathy.

My dad took the next step in building out our administrative team, hiring Marcia Ciarlo away from Oakland Scavenger's customer service department to join the firm as a staff accountant. As Marcia developed in her career, Tom and my dad saw her growth potential and, in 1989, they offered her a promotion to a new position as Firm Administrator.

"I was naïve when I started at the firm, just happy to have a good job," said Marcia. "My role was to move the administrative tasks away from the managing partner. It gave me a great sense of learning about the firm and how it worked. We were very simple and flew under the radar back then. We focused on providing great service."

Marcia has wonderful memories of this time at Armanino, Jones & Lombardi. "When we were pre-50 people, that was a special honeymoon period for the firm," Marcia said. "We had two extremely humble offices – one was actually a converted house. When we needed to meet with someone in the other building, we ducked through a hole in the fence to go between them."

"Andy Sr. was a tremendous mentor and always challenged me as Firm Administrator. He helped me evolve. When something new came up like handling construction of the 250 Juana building, he'd look at me over his glasses and he'd ask, 'How do you think you're going to do that?' It was a great incentive – I never felt afraid to roll up my sleeves and learn things," said Marcia.

MILLION DOLLAR FIRM

Constantly looking for new ways to grow the business, Tom completed Chris Frederiksen's "How to Build a Million Dollar Practice" course in 1980. At that time, there was a deep chasm between the Big 8 and all the small firms and sole practitioners in the industry. Below the Big 8, there weren't too many million-dollar practices, so Chris Frederiksen was ahead of his time. He told his seminar students that the image they presented to their clients was directly related to types of engagements and number of new clients they could win.

Empowered by the experience, Tom returned to the office and told Dad, "We can do that."

One of the lessons Tom took from the course was that those who wanted to be successful at business development needed to dress for that success. He immediately changed the Armanino, Jones & Lombardi dress code that consisted of bell-bottom jeans, satin shirts, wide lapels, and gold chains.

"We had always been a casual office, wearing whatever we wanted," said Cathy. "At Tom's request, the women started wearing dresses and pantyhose and the men wore button down shirts, jackets and dress slacks. It was a new look and feel for the firm, but we were all willing to support Tom."

Tom also got to take advantage of Chris Fredrickson's proprietary technological advancement. He had a keypunch machine and firms that completed his seminar got to submit client data to Chris whose machine would produce financials, eliminating the need to type them out on a typewriter. This is an early example of the firm's commitment to continuous improvement that enabled better client service.

The firm's profitability back then is to be envied today – they grew their profit margin to 52 percent with attention to high chargeability and high realization. True to Tom's aspiration, Armanino, Jones & Lombardi achieved one million dollars in annual revenue in 1982.

In 1984, Jeff Soulages, who had been our first accounting intern while a student at San Jose State University, walked back through the firm's doors after a year working at a software company. He had the biggest heart and making everyone successful was his constant focus. Jeff's professional expertise centered on technology – he introduced Armanino to our first word processing equipment, our first deployment of Microsoft software, and then followed that up with our first fax machine and a new, versatile copier machine.

"Jeff helped us move away from sending tax returns out to a service and waiting for them to be processed and returned," said Cathy. "He gave us the tools to be more efficient for our clients."

In 1989, Paul Bottini purchased a trucking manufacturing business from one of his clients and Jeff took over his computer hardware and software client base. Jeff and Nancy shared both an office and the same teaming ethic that my dad and Tom always held.

"Jeff was so mellow. We'd go out to potential clients, and I never had to worry, 'Would I need to give part of my billings to him?'" said Nancy. "We didn't have to think about that like they did at the big firms."

THIS PLACE IS GOING TO BE SPECIAL

In 1987, I graduated from Santa Clara University with an accounting degree. I picked Arthur Young among the Big 8 offers I had received because it was known as "the technology firm" at the time. Working with the best of the best there, it was an exciting time. That same year, my childhood friend and Tom Jones' son, Dan, went to Armanino, Jones & Lombardi for an informational interview. As Tom tells it, "I was trying to give Dan an example of interviewing for a job. He met with Andy Sr., and he hired Dan on the spot!"

Over at Arthur Young, I was working on Intel. Back then, Intel and Apple were the two accounts people wanted to work on – they were relatively small at the time, but we all knew they were going to grow. I learned a lot from a group of people at Arthur Young who challenged me. That said, the Big 8 top-down approach frustrated me, and it was at this exact time that I thought about leaving.

While working on consolidation spreadsheets that required complex technical accounting one evening, I fell asleep at 2 am in an Intel conference room. The partner on the job came in the next morning and lit my work papers on fire, reducing my hard work to ashes. He said, "Kid, nothing's that important. Go home, shower and get some sleep."

At the time, there were rumors in the industry that none of the work you did mattered, that partners approved work papers with little review for accuracy. The client was king and the end goal for accounting firms was to get the client's sign-off on the work. That's the reason I didn't think the Big 8 was for me. I wanted to work on things that mattered. I left because I wanted to make a difference.

Four of us staffers on the Intel team thought about starting our own firm. We met my dad for lunch to get his advice. He said, "You're all really smart, but silly. I have a platform where you can do all the things you want to. Why don't all of you come help me grow this firm?"

Dave Shiell took my dad up on the offer right away. Three months later, Dave asked me to come help him build the audit practice. I never thought I'd work at Dad's firm. One of my mentors told me this would either be the best decision or the worst decision I'd make in my career, going to work for my dad. It turned out to be the most positive thing I could have done.

At my Arthur Young exit interview on October 17, 1989 (the day of the Great Earthquake), I was told, "Armanino, we knew you would leave. You're too entrepreneurial for us." I took that as a huge indictment against the Big 8 and I hoped no one would ever leave Armanino because they were too entrepreneurial.

"Our firm goal has always been about creating opportunity for the younger people. We've been very people-focused from early on," said tax partner Dan Jones. "My dad taught me how to succeed and treat people with respect. He and Andy Sr. wanted you to improve, and they both had this unique ability and humbleness. They were never afraid of the up and comers. That's a legacy that we try to live up to today."

"This place is going to be special" – that's what I thought when I walked in on my first day. There was a hole in our profession. The Big 8, these huge firms, were starting to merge. Then, there were these tiny firms picking up the scraps from the big firms – they just existed. We realized there was big opportunity to grow into the middle.

Our firm had the vision that we could become incredibly valuable to our clients. I give our founders credit for that vision. They told us, "We're a team. We're going to really care about these clients." And the firm kept growing and adding talent.

When I joined the firm, there were 25 people, and we all did everything. Dad was given the title "Andy Sr." to help everyone distinguish between the two of us. We had a retreat in Lake Tahoe that year and everyone was asked how much they thought the firm would grow in the next five years. When I stood up and said, "We're going to double to 50 people," everyone in the room just laughed.

At the time, I was 25 years old, and Dave was 28. My dad asked us to run the Audit department with just a couple of people. He gave us some deference and told us, "You know what you're doing. You guys grow it, or you'll have to go back to the Big 8."

Dave told me he was amazed at how much "rope" my dad gave him back then. "Within a year or two, he let me take over a pretty big engagement," Dave said. "He empowered me by setting high expectations in terms of accuracy and how to work with his client. As accountants, all of us are control freaks by nature. It says a lot that Andy Sr. could have confidence and let me go."

This was the perfect scenario for me. I was not afraid of working hard and taking risks. I was not afraid of failing. We were thrown to the fire, but I learned more in that first year at Armanino, Jones & Lombardi than I did the whole time I was at the Big 8.

I've always been an avid reader and, at this point in my career, I became obsessed with improving my sales skills. One book advised to keep a log of every "No" you received in your sales efforts. By tracking the "Nos" and understanding why you didn't win, eventually, you would start hearing "Yes." So, I built out a spreadsheet and diligently tracked every potential client who turned me down.

One evening, as my dad was leaving the office, he stopped at my desk, looked over my shoulder and asked what I was doing. I explained my approach, and the man who had built a business by outhustling the competition just shook his head, chuckled, and left me with my spreadsheet. I learned a lot by recording my success and eventually, the "Yes" answers outnumbered the "Nos."

Two months later, Brad Cless was hired away from Arthur Young to join our tax practice. He came to Armanino, Jones & Lombardi for the great growth opportunity he saw with us.

"I didn't want to be at a huge firm that was so removed from the client experience," said Brad. "I wanted to get my feet on the ground and have a meaningful impact with my clients."

Brad and I became brothers-in-arms. We partnered together on hundreds of business calls. Brad and I learned how to use each other's strengths and, eventually, became very successful together.

A TRANSFORMATIONAL WIN

There is one particular "Yes" that stands out to me as the turning point for my approach to growing the business. For the first time, the Diocese of Oakland was going out to bid for an audit of their Catholic schools. They had 52 schools and a variety of other entities. The firms bidding on the work were BDO, two of the Big 8, and Armanino, Jones & Lombardi.

My wife Denise taught at one of the Diocesan schools, St. Paschal Baylon School, and I knew the principal. I talked with her and she didn't know much about accounting. She introduced me to a couple more principals, including Kathleen Radecke. I realized it was the same at all the schools – they didn't have controls in place that would allow them to be audited. Their accounting was rudimentary and messy, and the schools were not ready for an audit. They needed more basic accounting help.

Our competitors did what the Diocese had asked for by answering the standard audit proposal questions. Armanino had nothing to lose, so we bid a different type of engagement based on what I had learned.

Our presentation to the Diocese of Oakland focused on how we would help them establish internal controls and a standard chart of accounts for all their schools. We offered to include seminars on the basics of accounting for their principals and priests.

"I went into these audit interviews thinking there's no way we're going to hire Armanino," Sister Rosemary Hennessy, superintendent of the diocesan schools told me that day. "You were the smallest firm. I can't believe it, young man, we're going to hire you. You understood us and no one else did."

This win formed a belief that we could do things differently if we listened to our clients. We would provide what the clients wanted; not what other people told them they needed. It was transformational – we took an approach that was different from everyone else. If we had followed the standard proposal formula, we would have lost. We wouldn't have been able to stand out. This changed everything. This was the case study I used for the next 20 years as the business development trainer for the firm.

The Diocese of Oakland was a huge account for us, and we are still working for them today. This win launched our nonprofit practice at the firm. Not long afterwards, we added Paul O'Grady to the team.

"I was empowered to grow the nonprofit group," said Paul. "It was almost a startup culture in our early headquarters in San Leandro. We had no fear and a great sense of entrepreneurialism. The partners moved you very quickly if you demonstrated you could do it. I felt that people were valued for what they brought to the firm as opposed to how long they'd been there."

Another team member who joined in the early 90s was Bill Brause. He was working for Bank of America but played on our firm's softball team. When we finally convinced him to interview with us, he saw a big contrast between our firm's model and those of our competitors.

"In college, the Big 8 was everything. They never treated you the way you should treat a person when you interviewed with them – it was very 'Ivory Tower,'" said Bill, who became an audit partner. "When I joined Armanino, Jones & Lombardi, I realized this firm was different, and they were killing it."

"I saw that you could do all this entrepreneurial work in a hugely successful firm. We had a mindset I didn't see at other firms. We had a core group of young people and the older guys got out of our way when we were fired up about making it big," said Bill.

It wasn't all easy going in those days. Dad and Tom adopted a "good cop/bad cop" approach to running the business. My dad drilled down on the realization metrics and ensured everyone put in their maximum billable hours. He met with every biller every month. He held you accountable to bill and collect every hour. Tom's sense of humor and commitment to having a good time kept us all motivated.

Another special motivator was Nancy Koo, who we often turned to for advice. Nancy was a patient sounding board.

"I was known as 'The Ambassador,'" said retired partner Nancy. "The staff could always come and talk to me. I would look after their interests and I had the firm's interests at heart. I gave all of myself to be there for the clients and the firm. When you love your job, it's not your job. You want to be there."

It's important to note that Nancy raised a son during her tenure at Armanino. When I asked her how she balanced her commitment to our firm and to her family, she said, "I think the new saying is 'quality time.' It's not how much time parents spend with their children, it's the quality of that time. I tell other working parents to love their kids, care for them and teach them your values."

Back then, a typical hour-long firm management meeting would start with my dad in an all-business mode. He'd share our profitability metrics and our goals for the coming quarter. He used these opportunities to drive home the message that exceptional client service and proper billing were critical to our success. Meanwhile, Dan would sit to the side, drawing what we called "Dan Art." They were spot-on, hilarious caricatures of my dad and other firm leaders that captured the passionate debates they had about the best ways to run the business and keep the success going.

As Dad wrapped up the business portion of the meeting, Tom would find the opportunity to tell a joke, then another, and another, until we were all laughing so hard, we had to adjourn.

Then, it was back to work, copies of Dan Art tucked in our notepads, Dad's encouragement ringing in our ears, and smiles on our faces from Tom's jokes.

KEEP THE MACHINE GOING

While our young team members were focused on specific growth areas, Joe Moore became increasingly vital to the complete management of the firm. Having spent his whole accounting career at the company, he had soaked up our client service mantra and made the most of all the time he spent working onsite with our clients.

Joe told me that one of his favorite memories was the 1996 Christmas party. "I got to tell everyone at the firm that our $300,000 proposal to Recology was accepted. It was the biggest bid the firm had ever won," Joe said. "We did waste analysis for every aspect of the city of San Francisco. All our experience in solid waste paid off and this eventually became a two-million-dollar total engagement."

I always saw Joe as a great example of servant leadership. We had a term for his work style in the office – "Getting Schmoed" meant working a long day (and sometimes, a long night) with Joe on a client. But here's the thing. I had so much respect for Joe staying by my side, ensuring that together we delivered the highest quality work for our client. When I compared that experience to the Arthur Young partner who burned my work papers because they had no value, I knew I made the right decision to come work at Armanino, Jones & Lombardi.

By now, my dad and Tom were so proud of the organization they had built. Gratified with their success, they made the decision to retire at an early age. Tom Jones retired with fanfare in 1994 at the age of 54 at a surprise party his daughter, Lori Colvin, organized to honor him.

"My retirement party was a lot of fun," said Tom. "I remember thanking each individual and saying how much they meant to me."

My dad was 54 when he retired two years later. He always thought of his retirement party as the highlight of his career. So many of his clients stood up and talked about how he had helped them achieve their goals.

"It was a wonderful event that capped off an ideal career," said Andy Sr. "I got to deal with so many clients that were good people. It suited me."

Both their retirement parties were tremendous celebrations of what Tom and my dad had accomplished and the foundation they had built.

When Dad retired, Joe Moore was the right person to replace him, and I became Joe's right-hand man. I had made partner at age 29, the year before, and I was honored to support him in running the firm. Joe believed in working hard and adhering to certain metrics. He had a belief in big accounts that were really business consulting projects, not simply audit or tax work. Joe focused on what would really help the client build their business and this was the origin of our consulting practice.

"When I was taking over as managing partner, we had a machine. I wanted to keep it going along with Andy, Jeff and Nancy Koo, our other partners," said Joe. "Dave, Brad and Bill were all growing the practice then, too."

One of the wildest ways we delivered client value back then was a unique audit process for our solid waste clients. Joe recognized that garbage customers often got away with paying less than their fair share for their service, either because they piled too much garbage into and around their containers, or they used larger containers than they were billed for. Why not conduct field audits to ensure our garbage clients were properly billing their clients for the full value they received?

Imagine a world where digital cameras, smart devices and apps did not exist. Joe's great idea meant that Bill Brause and I would physically run down the street at 4 am ahead of the garbage trucks, take photos of overflowing trash cans with a film camera, and return to the office with the evidence. Our IT manager at the time, Doug Miller, built a computer program that could compile the data we collected and produce reports for our clients. They compared our report to their billing records and immediately corrected all the errors. This produced revenue for the clients, and they got really excited about it. Bill and I wised up after a few months and delegated the field audit to our younger interns – they really loved this particular Garbage Guys assignment!

Joe also kept an eye out for inorganic growth opportunities that would strengthen the practice. "We were always buying a practice and merging in a firm," he said. "We benefited, but the people we brought in would benefit, too. It had to work for everyone. We were always planning to succeed and keep growing."

During this period, the lead partner of Kimbell, McKenna & von Kaschnitz, Jim McKenna, would take me to lunch once a year and try to convince me and Joe to merge in his firm. In 1998, he told me, "You guys are going to do something special. I'll make you a hell of a deal – I just want my name on the firm."

The price was great for us and Joe agreed to the deal. Kimbell, McKenna & von Kaschnitz was the first firm of similar size to merge with Armanino, Jones & Lombardi and our official name changed to Armanino McKenna. The merger turned into a great success for us and our clients.

"Kimbell needed a younger firm like us," said Joe. "When we merged in a practice, it was not haphazard. We wanted it to be a win-win for the people joining us and we always wanted to get good staff. We promoted them all and their team did way better with us."

Around this time, my co-leader of the audit practice, Dave Shiell, came to a turning point in his career. His heart was not in the financial statement reviews nor in the day-to-day work of the department. Rather than leave the firm, he raised his hand to launch something entirely different for our clients – financial advisory services. We named the new division Financial Horizons and Dave was the sole employee.

"I was in my late 30s and really feeling it out, figuring out how to grow this new practice," said Dave. "Andy was supportive the entire way. He referred his important clients to me and that really meant a lot in those first days."

Dave's emboldened act to launch this new practice area paid off. Financial Horizons' name changed to Intersect Capital and the advisory firm has grown tremendously over the years. At the writing of this book, the team had $1.6 billion in asset management.

For thirty years, our firm had been one of the best kept secrets in the industry. I was convinced that our firm needed to join the small wave of CPA firms who were using professional marketing to grow their businesses in 1999. Prior to this time, it had been illegal, and then considered untasteful, for professional service firms to advertise their services. We interviewed several candidates for an in-house marketer position, but they just didn't seem to understand the opportunities we had to grow our accounting practice. I reached out to Dan's sister and Tom Jones' daughter, Lori Colvin, who was a marketing professional in San Francisco.

"Andy called me to get some insights and I walked through how I would approach the situation," said Lori. "Armanino hired me because I provided them with a different perspective than the other candidates had offered. I remember creating paper flyers in our little house office in San Leandro when I first started. It was so exciting to look to the future and think about who we could become."

Just two years later, Joe was approached by a 12-person firm called Armstrong-Gilmour. Our audit practice had expanded so much that we were now leading the firm. When Joe told me about the potential deal, I was enthusiastic about the additional tax practitioners we'd gain but told him we didn't need any more auditors. We had a great pipeline of up-and-comers and I wanted to make sure that they made partner. Joe simply said, "Go talk to Tom Gard."

I talked to Tom Gard, leader of Armstrong-Gilmour's audit practice, for a couple of hours and was convinced. He had the same beliefs and values that we did, and we moved forward with the merger.

"When I met with Armanino, I recognized I'd be going from being a big fish in a small pond to a small fish in a big pond. The firm was huge – it was 100 people at that time!" said retired partner Tom Gard. "A lot of firms will put up inhibitors like you're not allowed to be in leadership for a few years. That's just never been an issue at Armanino."

Tom Gard helped me strategize about continuing the growth of our audit practice and we named him to the firm's Executive Committee in that first year. We also brought on board a young audit staffer named Josh Nevarez who would grow to lead our private education audit practice as a partner in future years.

"Armanino is very open to talent that comes in, allowing them to run and not trying to hold them back," said Tom Gard. "For people who wanted to drive ahead, there were opportunities. I really felt a part of the firm very quickly."

Joe recognized the importance of continuing to build out our administration to manage the complexity of a growing team. Up to that point, Marcia and Cathy had always managed the human resources function. We interviewed several candidates and selected Vickie Moul as the firm's first HR Manager.

"My little dream was that I wanted a career that would allow me to balance being a mom with working," said Vickie. "When I joined Armanino, I was hopeful it would grow and develop into more. It seemed exciting."

I'm sure Vickie didn't realize just how exciting we would become, in part because of forces outside the firm. In 2001, the Enron scandal and the subsequent collapse of Arthur Andersen shook the accounting industry to its core. As the *Journal of Accountancy* recounted,

> "On the surface, the motives and attitudes behind decisions and events leading to Enron's eventual downfall appear simple enough: individual and collective greed born in an atmosphere of market euphoria and corporate arrogance.... Methods the company used to disclose (or creatively obscure) its complicated financial dealings were erroneous and, in the view of some, downright deceptive. The company's lack of transparency in reporting its financial affairs, followed by financial restatements disclosing billions of dollars of omitted liabilities and losses, contributed to its demise. The whole affair happened under the watchful eye of Arthur Andersen LLP, which kept a whole floor of auditors assigned at Enron year-round."

Armanino McKenna was perfectly positioned for this cataclysmic moment.

"It was a matter of being the right size and in the right place at the right time. We were in that sweet spot because there were not too many firms as large as us in the Bay Area," said Joe. "All of a sudden, some of that work moved down to us from the big firms. It wasn't haphazard or luck. We were planning our growth, always looking for opportunities, and a lot of other firms couldn't do what we were doing."

At this same time, Cathy Thomas, one of my high school classmates, called me to say she was leaving Deloitte. She joined Armanino McKenna to set up a consultative offering for companies that were required to comply with the Sarbanes-Oxley (SOX) Act. This legislation was passed by Congress at lightning speed a year after the Enron scandal broke to provide controls and avert any future, similar corporate misconduct. The practice boomed. Cathy built a team that included Dave Davis, who had a long career as controller and CFO for public companies. Cathy did a great job helping the firm to exploit this perfect opportunity to add public clients to our roster and grow the firm.

We also asked Tom Mescall to bring his technology product marketing and strategy expertise to the firm and help us grow our consulting practice. While Joe focused his interview questions with Tom on how many billable hours he would log, Tom concentrated on the strategic investments we needed to make to create an industry-leading technology consulting practice.

"I took the key learnings from my career and brought them with me to Armanino," said Tom Mescall, who had been a leader at PeopleSoft and Comergent Technology. "I saw the opportunity to partner with a technology leader who had a presence in the market. In 2004, Microsoft was not the most established business process software leader. But we made the right bet, as time would tell."

Joe took Armanino McKenna to the next level, really moving us into that mid-tier regional firm we had aspired to become. His leadership showed the fruits of firm investments made over those eight years in new acquisitions, lateral partners, marketing, and administration.

When Joe set aside his shovel and picked up his ledger full-time, the firm had seven team members. When he completed his term as managing partner 27 years later, we were 150 people strong and positioned to make an even bigger impact on the accounting industry.

OUR CLIENTS AND OUR PEOPLE – THE BEDROCK OF ARMANINO'S SUCCESS

Armanino's founders left the Big 8 with the goal of creating a firm where everyone felt valued and understood their contributions to the firm's success. My dad and Tom Jones sought to serve as a part of each client's team in driving them forward to achieve their unique goals. They also wanted to empower their employees by giving them opportunities to learn and grow professionally, all the while standing behind them with unfailing support. Their confidence in striking out on their own was rooted in the same empowerment that drives Armanino forward farther and faster than our competitors today. Joe Moore built upon this successful business model, creating greater growth opportunities, and making way for younger partners to pave their own paths to success.

"I'm proud that we built a business that allowed us to have a job we enjoyed. I looked forward to going to work almost every day, wrapping my arms around my clients, and helping them achieve their dreams," my dad said.

"We really had an equal opportunity practice for our employees – women and men," said Tom Jones. "We were very conscious of people's aspirations, where they wanted to go, and we created a path for them. We saw the quality of younger team members. There was no way we were going to sit on that.

"I was really conscious of letting people be who they were. Maybe I didn't agree with what they were doing, but I let them be who they were and didn't try to mold anybody in my image," Tom Jones said.

"The souls of its leaders permeate an organization," said Anton Colella, CEO of the Moore Global accounting firm network. "Armanino is the most respectable and respected accountancy firm in the world. It exemplifies the reason we should preserve firms with their own identity.

"You cannot erase the influence of a founder and a successor. The foundation is not an end to itself, but it is established to build something greater upon. What comes after it depends on the spirit and the passion of the founder," said Anton.

My dad, Tom Jones and Joe ran the business with integrity and the system they built created trust across the organization. They showed it was possible to move from the Big 8 model of individual success and pivot to collective entrepreneurialism. We have never feared risk-taking in an industry that is petrified of making mistakes. The original set of values empowered our team and created the growth that carried the firm from two accountants to 150. In 2004, Armanino McKenna was ranked the largest firm in the East Bay and the 88th largest firm in America by Accounting Today with revenues of $19.2 million.

As my dad and Tom like to say, they cleared the land and built the foundation for the skyscraper that was to come.

Marcia Ciarlo & Cathy Harrington Wilkinson

Firm First

It's not possible to talk about Armanino without referencing Marcia and Cathy. It is equally impossible to talk about Cathy without Marcia and vice versa. They shared 36 years serving at the center of our Armanino universe and we stretched them both as the firm grew. No detail was too small, nor any deal too large to be executed without their support. My dad and Tom Jones had a vision for building a firm that helped clients and employees realize their dreams, and Cathy and Marcia made so much of that possible.

CATHY

Cathy grew up with the firm, both personally and professionally. From her role as one of our first administrative assistants in the 70s to today, where she oversees administration of the Armanino Foundation and connects retired Armanino partners and former employees with the firm, Cathy has always wanted the best for the firm. And she's taken on challenges neither of us could have imagined. She and I were a team, and she made me a better managing partner and CEO by keeping me organized and prepared. Maybe most importantly, Cathy was a trusted team member who could challenge me and force me to articulate why we were growing so much and so fast.

"I did challenge both Andy Sr. and Andy, asking them, 'Why do we have to keep growing?'" said Cathy. "When I stopped and took myself out of the picture, I realized it wasn't about me and my comfort level with keeping things the way they were. It was about the opportunities all this growth brought to others at the firm.

"I am proud to have helped grow the administrative team and to make sure they're maintaining the quality of product the firm is putting out. Additionally, Andy and Matt Armanino challenged me to move out of my comfort zone and take over managing The Great Give. This annual day of hands-on service gives all our employees the chance to leave their laptops and email at their desks and go out into the community to volunteer. It takes a lot of coordination between the nonprofits we serve and our team members, but it makes me proud to see how it has grown over the years.

"I'm blessed to work with my sister Theresa Harrington, a manager in our Finance department, and so many lifelong friends every day. It's enjoyable to work side by side with people who want to make the firm a better place, not just for themselves, but for the young people coming up."

Cathy Harrington Wilkinson,
Administrative Assistant to Director of Administration to Director of Foundation and Community Affairs

Joined Armanino: 1978; Cathy remains a Firm First leader today

MARCIA

Marcia transitioned with all the firm leaders and had to change with each one. She was in charge of so much. I called her the "policeman" and she served fearlessly in that role. If someone got out of line with what we felt was ethically or morally right for the firm, Marcia

played a key role in detecting it and ensuring we held partners and staff accountable. When I served as managing partner, Marcia was one of the people I respected most because she had a humbleness to her leadership. When she spoke up, it was important, and I listened.

"As the firm grew organically and through mergers, it was a really challenging time," said Marcia. "We were very lean on infrastructure, but it made us all stronger. We worked together, we worked hard, and we accomplished a lot because we needed to. There was that culture instilled from the very, very beginning of empowering the staff and making them feel they're part of the process.

"I believe there is a soul to the firm, and the individuals who have catapulted the firm forward were looking more at the firm itself and not at how their efforts were going to help them individually.

"I feel we were, and still are, a family. I get this wonderful sense of warmth and love in my heart when I think about Armanino. It was just magical, and I'm extremely proud and lucky to have accepted that offer from Andy Sr. to come to work for them all those years ago."

Marcia Ciarlo,
Office Manager to Firm Administrator to Director of Finance

Joined Armanino: 1978; Marcia retired in 2014

02

Never Satisfied

2005-2014 | By Andy Armanino

> "Risk-taking, diversification, and not being satisfied – that defines Armanino. If you're satisfied, you're not motivated to grow, to add new people, new services and new geographies."
>
> - Tom Mescall, Partner

"Run faster, Andy. You've got to be faster, so much faster!!!" Kathy Jones hollered at me.

Catching my breath, I turned around and ran past the outdoor fountain at our headquarters in San Ramon again and again. Kathy wasn't satisfied until I was laying on the grass, fully spent. Before that, I had hung by a rope to scale the exterior of our office building, been in hand-to-hand combat with "ninjas" played by Dan Jones and Jeff Colvin, skateboarded through the parking lot, and received a "secret mission" in a pizza delivery box from Lori Colvin.

Anything to motivate our team to grow our business!

Tom Jones, our retired firm co-founder, filmed all the exploits and his wife, Kathy, served as the screenwriter, director, and producer. She turned the raw footage into a motivational 4-minute "Mission Possible" movie.

We rented out the Regal Hacienda Crossings theater in Dublin, California, so the entire firm could watch the short film together. After the laughter subsided, we used the opportunity to get everyone fired up about our new "Mission Possible" program. It was an internal contest to identify client needs and connect those clients with our experts in different practice areas. As the program brochure told our team: "You are not selling – you are secret agents finding out information, asking questions, and identifying opportunities to provide solutions for our clients!"

Then, we all enjoyed an advance screening of the 2006 "Mission Impossible 3" movie featuring Tom Cruise, a real action hero.

The launch event was raucous and in true Armanino McKenna fashion, the team left the movie theater energized to win cross-selling points for their designated teams. We signed nine new client engagement letters in the first month. One of our risk management clients hired us for valuation and tax services and sent the firm a thank you note for "being so responsive." That made all the running around our office complex to film our spoof worthwhile.

BAD BOYS AND GIRLS OF ACCOUNTING

I started my time as Managing Partner with raw energy. I was 39 years old, and ready to give it my all. That passion was fueled by my positive belief about who we were and what we could accomplish.

"Andy was like a tidal wave hitting Armanino McKenna," said Cathy Harrington Wilkinson. "We thought we were doing great before he became managing partner, but he had so much energy, everyone at the firm wanted to ride that wave."

I am a believer. I have a belief in people, in the power that we possess as people if we can unlock it, and in the goodness in people. I sought to unlock the potential of our people and, ultimately, of our firm. I was always talking about more lofty goals for Armanino McKenna. I clearly embraced what our founders and Joe Moore had stood for, but I was ambitious about what our firm might become and how that rapid growth would benefit our clients and our team.

We sought to claim a space in the industry for Armanino McKenna. No longer satisfied with being this "quiet little firm in San Leandro," internally or externally, we set big growth goals that would be difficult to achieve if no one knew of us outside our own backyard. So, we focused on building our brand recognition and our partners immediately recognized the value of these efforts. They supported all efforts to build a name for the firm.

The Armanino McKenna team was unafraid, unabashed, and hungry – my personal definition of modern cowboys and cowgirls. In 2005, we put our rapid growth plan into action and expanded beyond the East Bay through three business combinations. These transactions augmented our service offerings and brought us closer to our clients and the talent we sought to recruit in San Francisco and San Jose. By merging in Thibault Associates, a computer hardware and software reseller, we established Armanino McKenna as a full-service enterprise technology consulting firm. This put us on the map as a leading Microsoft software reseller and we never looked back.

Located so close to Silicon Valley where Forbes described the competition for talent as "intense" in 2005, Armanino McKenna was experiencing hiring pains of our own. Our "Recruit a Player" internal competition with the promise of cash bonuses for referrals got partners and staff excited to invite friends and colleagues to join our firm. By "gamifying" this strategic initiative, we gathered the names of 575 prospective employees and 321 resumes. We interviewed 47 of the candidates and made 17 crucial new hires in just 11 weeks.

That year, I also battled with one of my former Ernst & Young mentors to recruit Matt Perreault, a talented public company auditor, to our team. We had begun adding more public company and technology clients, but we didn't have the right expertise to continue expanding. Matt was the up-and-comer we needed to lead that effort. We told him all he needed to do was book one million dollars in new business and he'd become a partner.

"When I joined Armanino McKenna, it was about finding a culture match, folks that were very entrepreneurial," said Matt Perreault. "When I sold an engagement to complete three years' worth of audits in 100 days for Sigma Designs, the firm pulled together as a team to accomplish it. The audit, tax and consulting partners all came to me, said they realized how big this engagement was to the firm and they'd give me the resources I needed. I took real pride in working with such giving partners."

The CEO of Sigma later told us that our firm saved 800 jobs by completing that huge audit to help them refinance their debt. That's the kind of impact that keeps our clients coming back to us year after year.

"The people at Armanino have empathy and care for our clients," said tax partner Brad Cless. "It may seem like a cliché, but we're there for them in the good times and the bad times. Our very high client retention rate comes from their recognition that we're always thinking about them."

Our rapid growth strategy provided us with a broader set of offerings than other firms our size. Armanino McKenna was distinct in the industry, with our sights clearly set on serving the midmarket and corporate clients we were targeting.

Lori Colvin was empowered to launch creative marketing and internal communications campaigns. One theme was that Armanino McKenna partners offered more than just compliance advice. We provided our clients with business insights beyond a standard CPA's advice. Because our partners spent more time in the field with clients than our competitors, the clients benefited from a true relationship with us. We were always focused on helping them achieve their business goals.

Our advertising taglines included "Explore the Difference" and "Traditionally Untraditional" to set us apart from our more old-fashioned competitors.

"Nobody in the industry was advertising in the way that we were," said Lori. "Our firm approach was to never give up, always win. I would walk into Andy's office, proud of a recent marketing success, and he would always ask me what was next. I told him, 'Andy, you'll never be satisfied.'"

Lori was right. I never was satisfied because I never wanted us resting on our laurels.

Another tactic we used to get the firm noticed in the industry was speaking at accounting industry and business conferences. I took the opportunity onstage to share controversial positions on partner compensation, on branding and marketing, and on adding consulting services to traditional tax and audit engagements. My bold statements were tied to a consistent drumbeat. I was always leading with the theme that Armanino McKenna was different.

Armanino McKenna etched our "bad boys and girls" reputation in the industry by hiring teammates who went hard in the marketplace to win new clients and new engagements. This required us to look at independence all the time. We pushed the envelope on what we thought we could do, pairing our consulting services with audit and tax whenever possible.

Allan Koltin, advisor to the industry and recognized by Accounting Today as one of the top 100 most influential people in accounting for more than 20 years, immediately took notice of Armanino McKenna's alternative approach to firm management. He sought me out as a co-presenter to give his audiences a new, fresh perspective. During the first appearance with Allan, I outlined Armanino McKenna's unique partner compensation model.

At that time, all our partners participated in the annual compensation process. Everyone was in the same room, saw the same financials, and worked together to sort through the highs and lows of each partner's performance. Because we were focused on being a growth firm and we needed every partner's support, our compensation structure was set up to benefit both the firm and the partners.

We had two pieces of compensation. Our partners' current compensation rewarded them for what they did that year, rewarding high production, not the longevity of their tenure. The second compensation component was equity in the firm. Our partners benefitted from firmwide success and that promoted true ownership of the firm's strategic plan. Much like owning a stock, our approach encouraged Armanino McKenna partners to produce collective value. We would profit in the long run for our investments when we retired. Under this compensation model, all our young partners wanted to buy more equity. They sacrificed current year compensation to buy equity because they saw the ultimate value.

No other firm did this. The profession back then was very conservative. They compensated their partners based on length of service and individual books of business, effectively tying a conglomeration of solo practitioners into a firm rather than building a true team. Armanino McKenna was so radical from the other firms that I was scoffed at when I left the stage. Our peers said our model would never work.

Our model of true equity ownership for long-term firm growth was part of what attracted talent and accelerated our overall success. We used this unique compensation system to draw superstars in the profession away from the bigger firms to Armanino McKenna. They became part of our team and we experienced synergies that no other firm did.

"Armanino McKenna is a Disney story come true. If you can dream it, you can do it," said Allan Koltin. "They built something the accounting industry had never seen before. That made it almost like the perfect firm."

ALIGNING OUR STARS

Capitalizing on our newfound "fame," we kept up our expansion strategy via lateral hires and affiliation with a global accounting organization. We attracted young talent because of the message that Armanino McKenna was putting out in the marketplace about creating something special and different. Our new partners felt they could participate in building our firm, in making greatness happen here. That was a big piece of our early organic growth success.

In growing our firm with lateral hires, we employed the Aligning the Stars theory published by Jay Lorsch and Thomas J. Tierney. They identified stars not just as top performers based on past accomplishments, but, more importantly, as the team members with the highest potential to continue contributing to the firm's success.

> "Outstanding firms are consistently able to identify, attract and retain star performers; to get stars committed to their firm's strategy; to manage stars across geographic distance, business lines, and generations; to govern and lead so that both the organization and its stars prosper and feel rewarded. These capabilities are what give great firms their competitive advantage. Together, they constitute the work of aligning the stars.
>
> *Alignment* means creating organizational practices and structures that simultaneously fit the strategic requirements of the business and the needs of its key employees. Moreover, it is intuitively appealing: It makes sense that the more people in a company are motivated to perform in ways that achieve the company's goals, the greater the likelihood that the company will succeed."

At Armanino McKenna, we applied this alignment strategy to our recruitment efforts, and we landed the trifecta when Deloitte tax partners David Sordello, Jon Davies and Malcolm Ellerbe joined our team in 2006.

"The entrepreneurial spirit was much stronger here than in most accounting firms," said tax partner David Sordello. "Most CPAs don't live in a world where they want things to change, where they want to try new things. We were and still are always pushing boundaries, looking for something new to differentiate us."

"The main thing that drew all of us in was the opportunity to grow something from the ground up," said tax partner Jon Davies. "Armanino McKenna really had that culture of supporting entrepreneurship and innovation wholeheartedly, so we launched a corporate tax practice that gave clients an alternative to the Big 4 in the Bay Area."

These new tax partners sought a less bureaucratic structure that gave them the chance to interact directly with clients and deliver responsive, quick turnaround times.

"I was at David, Jon and Malcolm's orientation session, just six years into my career," said Dean Quiambao, an audit manager at the time. "I couldn't understand why they would leave the Big 4. They told me, 'We're here for the same reason that you're here. We see an amazing opportunity for the firm to grow and for us to connect with our clients like we couldn't at Deloitte.'"

That same year, Armanino McKenna made a tactical move to ensure our growing client base had the local and global support they needed to expand. Allan Koltin suggested we join a group of like-sized regional firms. As we all started sharing information, we immediately recognized the urgency to partner with an international network of accounting firms to meet our clients' needs and continue growing our businesses.

We were an attractive coalition of seven U.S. firms with nearly $250,000,000 in revenues for the international associations. We interviewed three different organizations and were most attracted to the people from Moore Stephens International Ltd. Once the paperwork was complete, our coalition of firms became the leaders of the Moore Stephens North America (MSNA) Board. Within two years, I was elected to the global board and have served there ever since.

Why did we need this international affiliation? Even small clients have international issues and questions. Without offices in financial centers around the world, we could not adequately service our clients and we risked being seen only as a local firm. The other big benefit for our firm is that our message of being a different type of fast-growing firm really resonated with our global partners. We got so much PR within the international Moore network that most of the foreign firms called Armanino McKenna with the U.S. work they had.

We brought smart, motivated people in to grow the firm rapidly. We created opportunity for our people through our affiliation with Moore Stephens and added new skillsets. Armanino McKenna filled a big gap in the marketplace through our expanded service offerings, growing talent pool and our commitment to having experienced team members in the field with our clients every day.

EDUCATING THE WHOLE PERSON

In 2007, Armanino McKenna's success allowed us to reimagine training for our teams. We knew it would pay huge dividends in the future. We were going to invest in our young professionals like no one else in the industry. We sought to continue our firm's profound support of up-and-comers and show them we believed they could accomplish more with us than any other firm.

This very deliberate investment came in two forms – empowering young leaders and building an internal professional development program like no other in the industry. First, I was inspired by an unusual speech I heard at an industry conference. The presenter was Rebecca Ryan, a young, redheaded economist and futurist, who stood visually and intellectually in striking contrast with her audience of managing partners, most of whom had gray hair. Rebecca spoke about the necessity to include strategic planning input from all levels of the organization to help "future-proof" your firm. She asked the audience to raise their hands if they had a staff advisory council. Not a single hand was raised.

When Rebecca stepped off stage, I was the first person at her side. "I'm going to do that – I'm going to launch a staff committee at Armanino McKenna!"

Rebecca replied with a laugh, "If you only knew how many times

I've heard that but never seen a leader act on it."

True to my word, I launched our Staff Advisory Board (SAB) as soon as I got back to the office. Staff members were nominated and voted on by their peers. We included representatives from all departments (tax, audit, consulting, and operations) and each of our offices.

"It was like a grammar school election," remembers Finance Manager Theresa Harrington with a laugh. "But when I won a seat on the SAB, I told myself with a sense of pride, 'If the people have voted for me, then I'll do it.'"

At our first meeting, I asked the group, "What's wrong with the firm?"

As expected, they were shy at first. Then I went to the whiteboard and wrote a couple of areas I thought we could improve. Little by little, the group started throwing out ideas. By the end of our first meeting, my hand was tired of writing and we had filled several whiteboards with their input. Before they left, the SAB was assigned to prioritize the top three things that needed to be addressed and we spent the rest of the year problem-solving together.

"We picked continuing education, communication from leadership and dress code as our top priorities," said Theresa. "'Casual Jeans Friday' was our claim to fame and it was a crowd pleaser. But I think we made a longer-lasting impact with our ideas around education and communication."

The SAB's request for more communication led to our leadership team spending more time in all the offices, walking the whole team through our 5-year strategic plan, and answering their questions about our goals for the future.

We were even more passionate about the SAB's request for continuing education. Their desire for professional development rang true with the words of industry authority David Maister: "Any firm that can outperform its competition in building and creating skills will gain a significant competitive advantage."

We decided that Armanino McKenna could build a top-notch learning and development department that trained the whole person. In addition to the technical training that is necessary for tax, audit, and consulting professionals to maintain their industry certifications, we devoted time, energy, and money into creating an amazing soft skills curriculum. Topics included the basics of communication, steps for conducting a productive business meeting, tips for writing effective emails, and myth-busting of generational differences in the workforce.

We wanted to establish a training program that we would really be proud of. We did a good job on the technical training, but we could beat anyone in training the whole person. We believed this would make our people better accountants, better consultants…even better people than their peers. We wanted to have better businesspeople than our competitors.

Some partners would say, "We're spending a lot of money on this. Shouldn't we just focus on technical training?" We stayed committed to our vision and kept making the business case for our comprehensive approach to training because we believed this was the right path for our future growth.

"We spent a lot of time on our people's skill development," said Dave Shiell. "We taught them to look for the client's pain and there would be opportunity for the firm to help address that pain. All this training helped us to deepen our client relationships."

"I've met a lot of Armanino people over the years," said client Mike Elam, former CFO of TerraMillenium. "The people I have interfaced with aren't just robots. They are people who really like each other and bring that positive mentality to their client work. They have high character and a team commitment to their clients that shows."

Futurist Rebecca Ryan visited our firm over the years to see our SAB and training programs in action. She said, "There's an edge, a shine to that Armanino personality. I've walked the halls in so many accounting firms and most people are head's down. At Armanino, your team members are head's up, they make eye contact, and they say, 'Hi.' That's a differentiator in this industry!"

With these investments in our staff, we once again stood apart from the rest of our industry who focused only on technical training. We marketed our unique professional development program and the Staff

Advisory Board at every college campus visit. We showed prospective hires that they could help make positive change at our firm and for their own careers.

"I would tell recruits, 'We've got really smart, really great people. You can tap into them and learn more at our firm because they want to help you grow and develop as a person,'" said Vickie Moul, Director/ Strategic People Partner. "At the Moore Stephens conferences, all the other HR leaders wanted to talk to me because I was from Armanino McKenna. I felt like a damn rock star!"

Of all the meetings I attended as a managing partner over the course of 15 years, some of my favorites were with the Staff Advisory Board. They energized me in equal measure to the empowerment we gave them to make us a better firm.

BEST OF TIMES/WORST OF TIMES

The longest years of my professional career were 2008 and 2009. Much like Charles Dickens' *A Tale of Two Cities*, Armanino McKenna made our way through the best of times and the worst of times. The rapid growth and unshakable optimism that were hallmarks of my first three years of leadership would be tested like I never imagined over the next two years.

Unaware of how long and deep the economic impact of the impending Recession would be felt by our clients, we launched into 2008 with aggressive growth plans, just like the previous three years. One of the first things we did that year was to strike a one-of-a-kind deal that would cement our bad boys and girls reputation in the industry. We added a public relations/marketing division to the firm, something no other accounting firm had ever done.

I'd like to say we really strategized and figured out that this was a great way to serve our clients' needs, but it didn't happen that way. Vintage Foster, who we'd built a relationship with while he was publisher at the *San Jose/Silicon Valley Business Journal*, was dropping off his personal tax payment to the firm when I ran into him in our lobby. He mentioned that he was thinking of leaving his newspaper role and starting his own business, so I invited him upstairs to my office. We went to my whiteboard, started working on costs, and I said, "Let's do it here."

Our business model to date had been to identify a client need and to go find an expert in the field to fill that need. In this instance, we thought we could find clients who needed Vintage's expertise. I told him, "I always bet on winners…and you're a winner."

"I thought it was the dumbest idea ever. But it was a trusting thing to do," said Vintage Foster, AMF Media Group partner. "Much like Andy sold audit to new clients in the beginning of his career, I kept selling and winning new business. Then, I would come back to the office and ask, 'How do we deliver this?'

"I wonder where my life would be if I hadn't bumped into Andy that day. Andy's confidence in me saw me through those initial years," said Vintage.

I don't think a division like AMF Media Group would work at most other firms. We identified this as a good opportunity because Armanino McKenna had been very aggressive in our own PR and marketing efforts, so we valued the skillsets Vintage and his team brought.

Unfortunately, the worst of times was right around the corner. The 2008-2009 Recession was the biggest financial setback in the firm's forty years in business.

> History.com tells us,
>
> The Great Recession was a global economic downturn that devastated world financial markets as well as the banking and real estate industries. The crisis led to increases in home mortgage foreclosures worldwide and caused millions of people to lose their life savings, their jobs and their homes . . . Although its effects were definitely global in nature, the Great Recession was most pronounced in the United States – where it originated as a result of the subprime mortgage crisis – and in Western Europe.

Prior to the Recession, Armanino McKenna's consulting, audit and tax practices were all experiencing double-digit compound annual growth rates. That year, it felt like we were stopped in our tracks. Our consulting business dropped 40% seemingly overnight and our tax and audit practices also suffered setbacks.

Knowing that we had to address the drop in our own business, our executive team got together many times. We set an original target for the number of layoffs we had to make, but as we reviewed the list and read through each name, we scaled back. In hindsight, we weren't prepared for the worst of the Recession.

Before the nation and our firm recovered, we realized we'd made a mistake and the first layoff wasn't deep enough, so we had to make a second round of staff cuts. Vickie tells this story best when she says that our leadership team took each layoff personally.

"To have to have those conversations with people that were part of the Armanino McKenna community was so hard," said Vickie Moul. "But we treated everyone as humans and did our best."

I felt this inability to foretell the future and the fiscal impact the Recession had on our business was a leadership flaw. The second round of layoffs created fear and distrust among our remaining team members, and the Executive Committee and I worked hard to win their trust back. Through it all, I had total support from other key leaders and the partnership. They understood that for the firm to make investments in our business, we needed cut deeply to position ourselves for the time ahead.

As 2008 was ending, we had more hard work to do to recover from the Recession, so I took the advice of my Young Presidents' Organization friends. (The Young Presidents' Organization is a collaborative professional development group for business principals who achieve significant leadership success at a young age.) They told me I needed a strong COO, that I couldn't keep inserting myself into every business decision. This was a proven path for success in corporate America, but a radical new idea for the accounting profession.

At other firms, people who are good at client service work also had to address firm operations as a side job. My vision was to build a world-class team of operations professionals that would support our accounting and consulting professionals. This would allow our partners to focus solely on our clients and our service delivery teams, not on the day-to-day of running the firm.

Once I embraced the idea, I knew just the person for the job: my younger brother Matt.

Matt began his career as an attorney in private practice, but after a couple of years, he left the professional services industry with disdain for the individual, siloed business model he witnessed there. He joined PeopleSoft in the mid-1990s when it gained international fame as a cutting-edge software company and rose from 200 to 8,000 employees. Then, Matt moved to WhereNet, a technology startup with no products and no team. After rewriting the business plan five separate times in the first couple of years, Matt and the leadership team grew it to a $50M company with several hundred employees. Soon, Zebra Technologies acquired WhereNet, and Matt worked for a year at the public company.

At the end of 2008, Matt was just back in California after spending four months on sabbatical in Europe with his family. He was exploring his next career move. One Sunday night during our weekly family dinner, I asked Matt to join the firm.

"On the way home, I told my wife Alexa that there was not a chance in the world I would do that," said Matt. "I didn't want to go back to the ugliness I had seen in professional services. I had a passion for building things, and I saw the strength that could be leveraged across a team in the technology industry to accomplish big goals."

Sunday after Sunday, I asked Matt to reconsider my offer. I was relentless and asked him to come in and meet Armanino McKenna's partners. Even though the firm was going through a lot of turmoil because of the Recession, all the partners made time to sit down with Matt and tell him what was special about the firm.

"I met with 25 people to vet out this opportunity. The firm had a growth culture, a clear commitment to growth. The vision was to grow bigger, better and be more impactful for our clients and our people," said Matt. "After that, I couldn't say 'No' to Andy anymore."

I'll admit, Matt and I had some bumpy times at first. There was initial reluctance to two Armaninos as CEO and COO. It was a big risk to bring Matt on, and I would have been held accountable if it didn't work out.

Despite any concerns at the outset, some of my favorite career moments came from watching Matt win people over because he cared, because he was so smart. He wasn't raised in the Armanino McKenna way professionally, but it didn't take long for him to live it in his daily interactions and prove himself.

During the Recession, our audit and tax departments weathered the storm by staying true to who we'd always been as a firm.

"In 2008-2009, our business development was slow to recover, but our culture recovered quickly," said audit partner Scott Copeland. "We stayed together, we supported each other. That is the testament for our culture."

"There are several reasons why we've fared well during recessions. Our leadership, our entrepreneurialism, our diverse practice, our desire to win – they all add up to our people coming together in this organization to get to a good place," said tax partner Brad Cless. "We're not smarter than anyone else, but we think through it and fight to get through. It's who we are – we're fighters."

In addition to Matt's firmwide operations responsibilities, he also brought deep technology industry expertise. Armanino McKenna was committed to growing our consulting practice and we asked him to team up with our consulting leader Tom Mescall to make that happen.

"I recognized our core value was our client relationships and knew we had the potential to be true companions to our clients because we understood the opportunities and challenges in their businesses," said Matt. "I witnessed deep care and humanity in our client relationships. This went back to my dad's original vision. With our SOX, outsourced accounting, and IT consulting services, we had the ability to take this privileged position, expand it and really engage with our clients."

Matt and Tom spent much of Matt's first year at the firm developing a long-term strategy for our consulting department. They identified the investments we needed to make for the future. Their vision was a unified consulting department, with IT consulting, SOX, outsourcing and technical accounting all available to our clients as a single solution.

TerraMillenium was an Emeryville client that grew right alongside Armanino McKenna and took full advantage of all the tax, audit, and consulting expertise our firm provided.

"We used a lot of services at Armanino. Our company started out 30 years ago with only 20 people, so initially, we just needed audit and tax services," said Mike Elam, retired CFO of TerraMillenium. Today, the privately held company has 4,500 employees and 26 offices across the United States.

"When we did a computer upgrade with Jeff Soulages, I appreciated the time and effort he spent on that. As we grew, I viewed Armanino as my most trusted advisor for the things that were at the top of my agenda. Whenever I needed something that I couldn't handle on my own, Armanino could do it," said Elam. "I only ever used Armanino."

In another industry first, Armanino McKenna developed a Chief Financial Officer survey and benchmarking study. The CFO Evolution® was a set of initiatives designed to "take the pulse" of CFOs on their responsibilities, roles, and strategic priorities within their organizations. Our survey revealed that CFOs were spending more than 55 percent of their time in the accountant role, 20 percent of their time as protectors of the business, and only 25 percent of their time as business leaders. But when they were asked how they desired to spend their time, CFOs turned those numbers upside down, seeking to spend at least 50 percent of their time leading growth initiatives for their organizations, like identifying acquisition targets, conducting market expansion research, and vetting out new geographies for market entry.

Armed with data from our CFO Evolution survey, Matt and Tom met face-to-face with 24 CFOs across the San Francisco Bay Area, from nonprofits and wineries to manufacturers and technology leaders. They benchmarked the individual companies against the best-in-class examples gleaned from our CFO Evolution survey data. They walked CFOs through ways to update or re-engineer their people organizations, their processes, and their technology solutions for greater efficiency. When CFOs started spending less time on the manual accountant role tasks, they were freed up to lead the critical initiatives their CEOs and Boards wanted them to focus on.

"The CFO Evolution helped make us healthier as an organization," said consulting partner Tom Mescall. "We decided to be closer to our clients to make sure we were being responsive. They got us through the Recession crisis – our clients."

Matt also helped me to reshape Armanino McKenna's internal systems, doing it piece by piece all the time. We recognized that the firm model we had in the beginning wasn't going to serve us well for the firm we were becoming.

For instance, we had to change processes to build out our consulting practice. Many people believe that Arthur Andersen's demise was all related to the Enron crisis. But industry insiders know that Arthur Andersen blew up because of infighting between audit and consulting partners about market share and compensation. We did not want the same thing to happen as Armanino McKenna expanded.

As consulting got larger and larger, we were proactive to avoid a blowup. We gave the consulting team a position in leadership and key decisions. We changed how we decided compensation to make sure consulting had a voice. We made it work.

Armanino McKenna also did something most firms never do. We changed our partnership agreement all the time. We recognized the constraints of the typical accounting firm governance model. We had a culture of trust and innovation that allowed us to experiment with new organizational structures and governance models. This was key to our future success.

"If we uncovered something that we could 'break' to make it incrementally better or more efficient, Andy and I would ask ourselves, 'Why not?'" said Matt Armanino. "We were always looking for opportunities to give ourselves an edge over the competition.

"Some people may not be attracted to our model, but we have people who self-select for Armanino McKenna. They can be superstars whose contributions make for a winning team. Like the Golden State Warriors' motto during their heyday, 'Strength in Numbers' represents our strategy.

Our superstars can excel and bring the power of other superstars to their clients," Matt said.

"This is a place where you can do your own thing in your own way, said tax partner David Sordello. "There's support and structure, but the firm also trusts people enough to empower them to do their own thing. If you're successful at that, it compounds and grows. It's collaborative – everyone is on the same team. We make business decisions that way, we hire that way."

When Matt joined the firm, I didn't feel alone in my leadership role anymore. I spent a lot more time thinking about strategy and I had a sounding board with Matt. And as I had been Joe Moore's right-hand man years before, Matt now stood side-by-side with me to work through the challenges of the Recession and position the firm for the future.

A couple more "best-of-times" moments of 2009 came from the launch of two internal programs. They each made our team feel so empowered, they remain critical components of who we are as a firm today. First, the Management Advisory Board (MAB) was established and became a vehicle for enhanced leadership training. Through a self-nomination process, this group of managers and directors are selected by our Executive Committee to implement programs that support the firm's strategic plan. We saw it as an informal "path" to promotion and partnership for our rising stars. One of my proudest moments as managing partner was when three of the original MAB members (Jeremy Sucharski, Theresa Brown, and Ricardo Martinez) were named partners all together in 2014.

The Great Give started out as a one-time event in May 2009. We closed all our offices and invited our staff and partners to work side-by-side on 16 community service projects around the Bay Area. We served breakfast at Glide Memorial in San Francisco, cleaned kennels at Tony LaRussa's Animal Rescue Foundation in Walnut Creek (and Tony came out to meet our team!), cleared paths on the grounds of the Eugene O'Neill National Historic Landmark in Danville, and much more.

One of the best outcomes was the natural collaboration that occurred with tax, audit, consulting and operations staff, managers, and partners, all mixed together at the different worksites. They were on equal ground to give back to the community. In the process, they came to know one another in new ways. We were all tired but so proud of what our team efforts had accomplished at the end of the day.

We had thrown a lot of fun Armanino McKenna parties over the years, but nothing came close to the enthusiasm we created with the Great Give. Our team clamored for us to repeat it the next year, and now, it has become an annual tradition where all firm employees are encouraged to nominate charities in their local communities for our day of service. Once the nonprofits get narrowed down to a final list, employees go to an online portal and select the nonprofit they will spend the day helping. The Great Give is so popular that the sign-up site often crashes temporarily under the crush of team members logging in at the same moment to pick their favorite charity!

Sadly, just as we came off the happy high of our first Great Give, tragedy struck. My friend and long-time Armanino McKenna partner Jeff Soulages died of a heart attack while coaching his son's Little League team. The entire firm mourned his passing and many, many of us attended his funeral in support of his wife and children. Jeff had always represented the best of our firm. He was a gentle spirit, always smiling, who exhibited his personal commitment to his clients and teammates in all his actions.

In the days after his death, we did our best to honor Jeff's legacy at the firm. Because he was always ready to lift up a team member and help them to develop professionally, we named our largest conference room in his honor: the Soulages Training Center. We also created the Jeff Soulages Values Award and every six months, honored a staff member or partner who exhibited one of Jeff's many qualities such as honesty, teamwork, positivity, compassion, and exemplary client service. Award winners were nominated by their fellow teammates and chosen by the firm's Executive Committee. We wanted Jeff's spirit and values to be carried on by the next generation of Armanino McKenna team members and this award was coveted by those who earned it.

MAKING OUR OWN LUCK

Armanino McKenna entered 2010 as the nation's 39th largest firm with 250 team members. After two long years of revenue decline and staff cuts, we needed something to rally around. Our team needed to regain our swagger. The MAB came through with one of the best internal rallying cries we ever had – "Top 25!" They wanted Armanino McKenna to join that elite group of the nation's 25 largest accounting firms.

The MAB worked with Rob DeMartini in our Marketing department to create wall-size graphics that went up overnight in all our offices. They built a program that included promotional internal emails, flyers, and videos to get the whole firm talking about this new milestone. I loved it. Anytime we were focused on rapid growth and climbing higher, it ignited that entrepreneurial fire inside me.

"Every firm says growth is important to them," said audit partner Scott Copeland. "But how many firms sit down every single day to do what it takes to grow? Armanino McKenna puts in that work to grow and build, but we do that through our relationships. We all care about each other, our clients and the firm."

Our corporate tax practice experienced a bit of a downturn in 2008 but bounced back and kept that growth machine going in 2010 and beyond. As a lower cost alternative to the Big 4, our value resonated in the marketplace.

"Our mission was directly aligned with what a lot of companies were looking for at that time and still are today – they want more value for their money when it comes to tax services," said corporate tax partner Jon Davies. "The clients who switched stayed with us after the Recession because of the service we provided them."

"I like to win, but winning is not just getting a new account," said tax partner Brad Cless. "It's coming up with a better outcome for our clients than somebody else did. It's providing opportunity for the people who work here. Those are the things that are really important about our growth."

When the consulting department was deeply struggling to succeed during the Great Recession, I remember stopping by to check in with Matt and Tom Mescall one night and asking, "You guys do know what you're doing, right?" Years later, Matt admitted to me that while they gave me an answer filled with confidence, he turned to Tom after I left and asked, "Do we know what we're doing?!?" Time and the economic recovery would prove their approach to be the right course for Armanino McKenna.

"One of the secrets of our firm's success is that I always felt support for our strategy of tying technology solutions to all of our consulting services," said Tom. "There were no undercurrents of second-guessing from other department heads. The firm's partners never wavered on this future vision for the firm."

"You need people who respect each other to make growth happen. Our whole executive group and partner group, we respected each other," said retired partner Tom Gard.

Armanino McKenna's ability to embrace different ideas, to support people, and to stay united, locked arm-in-arm, is a critical component to our rapid growth success. The firm invested in a future vision for the consulting department would require more acquisition investments.

We merged in 1 Source Solutions in San Jose on August 30, 2010, to become the West Coast's leading value-added reseller of Microsoft Dynamics software and one of the Top 10 Bay Area management consulting firms.

"It was never about just growing," said tax partner Dan Jones. "We were always adding something that was complementary to what we did or that brought in new skills. We wanted these transactions to be additive versus just numbers. Our North Star reason for acquisition was always moving us forward."

In 2012, cloud-based software was gaining a strong foothold in the marketplace. Cloud software, also known as Software-as-a-Service (SaaS), is hosted on the vendor's servers and accessed through a web browser. It is priced as a monthly or annual subscription, much like Apple Music or Netflix. This "new" software model (which originated in 1999 before the dotcom bust) quickly gained market share over on-premise software that is installed on a customer's own computers and servers and is considered a capital expenditure. Armanino McKenna set out to be a leader in the cloud software space, signing reseller partnerships with two fast-growing vendors, Intacct and Adaptive Insights. Combined with our organic growth in software consulting and strategic business combinations, Armanino's consulting revenues reached 50 percent of the firm's total income. We grew faster than our competitors because we understood the rewards that come from decisive action and we weren't limited to just our audit and tax business.

"We see inorganic growth as a way to accelerate things we're excited about," said Matt Armanino. "In order to have a strategic inorganic growth strategy, you have to have a strong organic growth strategy. We create our own success."

All this geographic and service expansion led our Executive Committee to reflect on our firm's brand in the marketplace. With AMF Media Group, our Chief Marketing Officer Lori Colvin led a competitive analysis project that revealed that most U.S. accounting firms promoted themselves solely on their own capabilities, services, and accolades. The research revealed the opportunity for our firm to stand apart from the crowd once again and we made the investment to rebrand.

This rebranding effort in 2013 took on several public-facing aspects of the firm. First, we decided to finally change our name to reflect what all our clients called us: Armanino. When I called Jim McKenna to share the news with him, he laughed and said, "I can't believe you kept my name this long!"

Next, we dropped the tagline "CPAs & Consultants" because we were bigger than that and didn't want to be limited in the services and products we could develop in the future. We chose bold orange and green accent colors that set us apart from the 75 percent of competitor firms who use the more conformist blue color in their logos.

Most importantly, we rewrote our website, firm brochure and all our sales materials to speak to the things our clients valued and not just about Armanino's capabilities. We shared stories of helping clients turn the financial insights we provided into action to grow their organizations.

Our firm brochure focused on the lifecycle needs of a company, from start-up and growth stages to exit strategies.

We closed out this era as a Top 25 firm with $130 million in annual revenues. We crushed our growth goal in 2014 and the partners unanimously agreed to throw the biggest party our firm had ever seen! We took over Castlewood Country Club in Pleasanton, California, and transformed it into a party zone. We had locations that offered massage stations, painting lessons, obstacle courses and soccer golf, yoga lessons, food and drink tasting stations…even a dance contest. But the ultimate surprise was when the sky lit up with fireworks, Smashmouth came onstage and the Armanino team sang and danced along to all their favorite 90s hits by the band!

PUSHING EACH OTHER UP THE HILL

I may have brought a passion for growth to the firm, but it took the empowerment of the whole team for us to reach these new heights. It may seem a juxtaposition, but by embracing our collective bad boys and girls reputation, we achieved universal commitment to the firm's growth goals. We're not competitive internally. We're competitive externally. We want to be on a winning team. The Armanino teamwork, pushing each other up the hill to higher heights, is the true success of this rapid pace of growth.

Most accounting firms never change their structure and systems. They operate in the same manner as they did 30, 40, 50 years ago. This is the Armanino differentiation. We kept changing processes and systems as we went. We weren't married to any one system. We were married to getting results for our clients and our firm. Challenging the status quo is what makes us different and what kept us moving forward even during the deep challenges of the Great Recession.

"Risk-taking, diversification, not being satisfied - that defines Armanino," said Tom Mescall. "If you're satisfied, you're not motivated to grow, to add new people, new services and new geographies."

PACKETFUSION

Packet Fusion

Positive Impact on Our Clients

My leadership era was launched with a deliberate goal for Armanino to become the industry's best, most exciting firm. We achieved that goal because of the tremendous positive impact it had for our clients and our people. Every expansion – service line, geographic and acquisition – brought greater opportunity for our people to work more closely with clients to deliver on their dreams. And it only got better from here.

In 2001, Matt Pingatore joined Pleasanton, California-based Packet Fusion, which had started as a telephony reseller. Matt's role as CEO and owner has transformed Packet Fusion into a consultative partner serving customers with a variety of technologies and support services.

Today, Packet Fusion serves as a trusted advisor to its clients, delivering unified communications and collaboration tools, call center technology and training, and elastic workforce capabilities. The new business models that Matt introduced created growth throughout the U.S., especially in California and Texas, for the firm. This growth brought a myriad of business challenges.

"When I joined Packet Fusion in 2001, we were experiencing some financial challenges," said Matt. "After I was reintroduced to my elementary schoolmates, Matt and Andy Armanino, and to Tom Mescall by mutual friends, Armanino came in and helped me fix things."

"Our companies started doing some business together. We talked about how the firm's technology consulting practice was growing to include things like CFO for hire. I used their interim CFO services and we continued expanding our relationship."

"Packet Fusion has now worked with Armanino since the early 2000s, on tax and outsourced accounting for eight years, and audit

Armanino Leadership Conference

Positive Impact on Our People

reviewed financials for three years. They also support our Microsoft Dynamics and Customer Engagement platform. We wouldn't have the single platform to run our business without the help of these guys. I love how Armanino works with us. It has been a very fruitful, strategic relationship and has supported our success."

"I like to attend Aramino's executive roundtables, conferences, and special events like the AI Lab launch. I particularly enjoy the bigger picture conversations. Armanino has the moxie and grit to make their thought leadership stand out, in words and actions."

"I wouldn't know who to trust for all the services we consume and, because Armanino is full service, I don't have to. As an Armanino client, we're part of a larger organization and can tap into the firm's expertise. I trust Aramino like our technology customers trust Packet Fusion, with the confidence that we are working with experts in their field, who have the experience to solve problems and the desire to help us continue to grow."

One of the best examples of our dedication to developing the whole person at Armanino starts before our professionals even join the firm. From its inception, Armanino's Leadership Conference has stood apart from standard recruiting events. Vickie Moul, our HR director, and Kevin Turco, one of our campus recruiters

at the time, developed the Armanino Leadership Conference in 2007 for college sophomores. It was different than Big 4 leadership programs where students were "sold" on the reasons they should pick a firm. Instead, Armanino's event facilitated relationship building between the students and our partners and staff.

"I was so impressed at how Armanino's top brass showed up and hung out with the students in their first experiences as potential employees," said Rebecca Ryan, who moderated the first conference as a favor to the firm. "And the key message at the event was 'Master your communication skills and how you show up.' Now, you can see it across the firm. You can talk to anyone at Armanino."

"I kept pushing for the Armanino Leadership Conference because we were always competing for talent with the Big 4," said Vickie Moul. "Our partners and staff were amazing. They actively participated with the students in our True Colors® personality assessment, and we focused on activities that empowered the students to become successful businesspeople."

The best way to understand the impact of Armanino's Leadership Conference is to see it through Bryan Vencill's eyes. Bryan was a Cal Poly sophomore who attended the first session. Fast forward 14 years, and he is now a CPA and partner with Armanino who volunteers his time each summer with the current generation of students.

"The first Leadership Conference was super unique, authentic…it felt personal," said Bryan Vencill. "I could see that people were having fun and were very excited to go to work at Armanino. I felt I could have

Striking a Balance

2015-2018 | By Andy Armanino

> "Everyone I've met at Armanino is on fire about the firm. When I visit your firm, I see people who want to be part of the 'Armanino Army.' The firm has defined its 'why' – as a successful organization, Armanino has a responsibility to give back and is so intentional about it, it permeates their souls."
>
> - Mike Platt, Principal of the Platt Group and Publisher of *Inside Public Accounting*

some success and make an impact here as an individual and on a team.

"The conference has morphed significantly from my session to where it is today. We've even created a virtual platform because of the pandemic. But one thing remains the same.

"At every conference, our leaders Andy and Matt have connected directly with the students, taking time to talk to them one-on-one. They share what the firm has to offer and show how much they love what they do. Armanino is not content to offer the same recruiting event that other firms do – we try to do it better and different.

"In 2007, I can't say that I knew I was going to stick it out in public accounting. Most students don't. But when you make partner at Armanino, it's just the start of a new journey. I never wanted to stand out in school, but now I want to stand out in the market. We want to show that we do things differently and we innovate. All the Armanino leaders continue to push forward and not be content with where we are today," concluded Bryan Vencill.

A valuable lesson in our pell-mell growth trajectory became a turning point for Armanino. It spurred us to articulate our reason for being.

With an appetite for more growth in Silicon Valley, we completed the Berger Lewis Accountancy Corporation acquisition, our largest to date. Berger Lewis' annual revenues of $12.5 million represented approximately ten percent of Armanino's annual revenues on the transaction date of January 1, 2015.

On paper, the transaction looked perfect. It meant a significant San Jose office presence and brought a large set of tax, audit, and outsourced accounting clients to the firm as well as a strong team of professionals. For the Berger Lewis leadership team, the transaction created the opportunity to expand their service offerings to their clients and provide greater professional development opportunities for their staff. But it was the off-ledger lesson that taught Armanino how important our culture is to our success.

Several months after the ink had dried, we realized that there were holdouts and people who wanted to keep doing things the way they

always had. They didn't understand the reason for some of Armanino's processes and, therefore, didn't appreciate the new ways they were asked to work. Some of the Berger Lewis partners were more traditional and restrained than the legacy Armanino partners. They did not speak up about the integration challenges they and their staff were experiencing. This meant that getting alignment around business processes and our joint future growth took much longer than we anticipated.

"For some people, it was more painful than others. Helping us to integrate right in the beginning proved difficult because we were still in our own office building," said Larry Kuechler, former Berger Lewis and retired Armanino partner. "Even when everybody's committed, when you come into a new culture and a new set of rules, you don't always know how to get stuff done in a positive way."

There came a point when tax partner David Sordello and I gathered all the San Jose partners, new and legacy, together in a conference room. We told the group, "We understand that we may not have been as clear as we should have been about who we are as a firm, but you're either with us or you're not." That was not an easy day, but the resulting discussions and cooperation were a great learning experience for me and our Executive Committee.

"The leaders have to be involved with keeping the troops energized during a merger," said former Berger Lewis and current Armanino partner Tom Bondi. "It helps to have partners communicate to the staff that it's going to be painful for a while, but it's worthwhile for the opportunities that will come."

Those painful conversations made us realize that we could have handled the Berger Lewis onboarding process better and we strove to improve for the future.

"This is part of our culture, being human enough, vulnerable enough to admit our missteps. I feel it's a true sign of success when our leaders are willing to acknowledge their weaknesses," said my brother Matt. "In this instance and so many others, we moved forward with strength together."

Because of Berger Lewis, Armanino re-framed how we brought firms

in and made them feel welcome. Now, we launch each transaction with a high-energy announcement event for everyone from the new firm to attend. The "merging in" team gets the chance to meet representatives from our Staff Advisory Board, our Management Advisory Board, all the way up to the highest levels of our partnership. We include time for questions and answers and have leaders from both firms discuss the benefits and opportunities the merger will create for everyone.

The weeks between the announcement event and the actual transaction date are occupied with a comprehensive onboarding process to transition our new team members, processes, and technology as seamlessly as possible. We provide opportunities for the new team members to join our committees and get involved in Armanino's culture beyond their client hours.

"Now that we all have taken a step back, we realize the Berger Lewis integration is how Armanino learned to get underway in its mergers," said Larry Kuechler. "In spite of some of the difficulties, the fact that we have as many people as we do who are still here is a testament to landing in a good place.

"I'm proud that we achieved what we hoped for in coming together. We got to become the growing firm we aspired to be and that created great opportunities for our people and our clients. Today, we are we – we became Armanino," said Larry Kuechler.

But far more important than improving the way in which we proactively managed future mergers was the realization that Armanino needed a better way to share and reinforce our values across the firm. How exactly did we manage both the professional "Smart Side" and the impassioned "Soul Side" of our business? This approach came so naturally for the team members who had grown up in the Armanino way. How could we make it tangible for the entire growing team?

I didn't want Armanino to be like all the other firms in the industry. Based on our interpretation of the writings of Pat Lencioni, David Maister and other business experts, and my daily leadership experiences, I believed we could not only be a growing, profitable firm, but also a very healthy organization. We could be so much more than the average

professional services firm. The more time I spent as managing partner, the more I knew this was what we were creating.

We strove to do a better job of articulating our core purpose as a firm. Our Executive Committee invested the time and energy necessary to make this happen. Before I tell that story, I'll define what both the "Smart Side" and the "Soul Side" mean to Armanino.

OUR SMART SIDE

Most accounting firms are high on the smart side, filled with technical people who are very comfortable with statistics and key business metrics. Our profession historically and, even today, spends a lot of time on the smart side of the business. Accounting firms are great at focusing on what is measurable, concrete and data driven. And our firm was no different. I salute that and I know it's important.

For instance, my dad demanded high utilization rates. He wanted every invoice collected. Every month, you had to explain your numbers if they weren't what was expected. All client work had to be billed and write-offs were almost non-existent back then. Joe Moore also emphasized utilization and hard work. He had gotten ahead in life by working hard and he believed that's how the firm should grow. Hard work is still important to us, but it doesn't tell the whole story of Armanino's success.

David Maister is the author of two seminal books for the industry, *Managing the Professional Service Firm* and *True Professionalism*. According to his formula, Armanino was doing great: "The profit from your practice is found via the simple multiplication of four key sub measures: margin, rate, utilization (also referred to as chargeability or billability), and leverage."

David Maister also taught that "if you value something, then you must monitor your performance in that area, accept nothing less than excellence, and actively work to learn what to do differently every time you fall short of excellence."

We were very profitable as a young firm during the years Dad and Joe were in charge. But we became more profitable as we grew. Marcia Ciarlo and our Executive Committee were crystal clear about the importance of tracking and reporting on key financial metrics. We knew every aspect of our profits and always strove for continuous improvement on the smart side.

Another way to measure the smart side of our business is to benchmark Armanino's performance against a peer group of accounting firms. Annually, we participate in the *Inside Public Accounting* Financial and Operational Report Card survey which has been the industry best practices standard bearer for more than 35 years.

From this objective, numbers-driven survey, the industry's "Best of the Best" rise to the top and Armanino is proud to have been listed among those top firms consistently for more than 15 years. The report card's four segments include the following categories and sample metrics:

Net Revenue – Net Revenue Per Charge Hour and Organic Growth Rate

Operations – Utilization and Accounts Receivable

Net Income – Net Income as a Percentage of Partner Revenue and Net Income Per Work Hour

Compensation – Average Equity & Non-Equity Partner Compensation and Average Professional Staff Compensation

The drawback with using a benchmark like the one produced by *Inside Public Accounting* is that not all firms have the same values. Armanino established growth goals that are balanced – 50 percent organic expansion and 50 percent inorganic expansion. We knew by going down this path that we would dilute some of the metrics our industry holds in high esteem. It's very hard for larger firms that are growing

geographically to meet the benchmarking standards. Acquisitions can diminish some of those numbers. We consider ourselves a different firm that is entrepreneurial and always investing in the future.

"When you gather the leaders of the accounting industry together, you find the top three topics about running their firms hasn't changed in over 30 years," said Michael Platt, the publisher of *Inside Public Accounting*. "They focus on partner accountability, partner succession planning and moving away from compliance work. Armanino is differentiated in that the firm has made a very direct movement from opportunistic growth to intentional, evolutionary growth. That is a unique characteristic in the industry."

Always focused on the opportunities Armanino was creating for our people, our leadership team believed that balancing the smart side of our business with the personal development of our team members was critical to the future of the firm.

WORK-LIFE INTERSECTIONS

I want to share two stories of personal evolution that illustrate how balancing the smart side and the soul side of the business can have deep personal value outside the office. Our audit partner Scott Copeland likes to say, "We are a unique firm that encourages our people to really be the best versions of themselves."

Unfortunately, I had to learn the hard way how to become the best version of myself.

For many, many years before I became managing partner and for the first five years of my leadership, I worked nonstop. Work was my top priority, and I spent an undue amount of time there. I loved it. I was energized by it. I felt very competent and there were so many positive things happening for us as a firm that it felt like the right thing to do.

Even though I wasn't a tax partner, my wife Denise and my oldest son Drew remember that I worked seven days a week from January to April 15th every year. There was too much of a bright line in our

family – Denise had the home stuff, and I had the work stuff. Raising kids was new and different and, honestly, I didn't feel as in control at home as I did at the office.

The transformational point in my life came when Denise told me this devotion to work wasn't going to work for our family. We split up off and on for a year. I did a lot of reflection and decided that I needed to change some of the priorities in my life. Work was really important, but my family and my relationship with my wife are the most important things to me.

After I came to this realization, I got more perspective on how to do the job of managing partner. This was the kickoff point for me to becoming a more inclusive leader, listening to more people, and trusting a lot more to the team. I recognized that others weren't going to do everything the way I would have done it and that was okay.

This was the right decision – I just had a hard time seeing it until there was a crisis. I was very fortunate that Denise decided to stick by me and work through this difficult time. Our firm goal is to empower our team to become better people. This time in my life helped me to recognize that we're all evolving all the time. In the end, it made me a happier, more complete person – a better version of myself, in Scott Copeland's words.

Another lesson of how our personal and professional lives intersect came from our audit partner Matt Perreault. He endured a painful divorce and a period of depression, but he was so grateful for how the firm supported him. Every partner offered to manage a few of Matt's clients for him so we could help him through that difficult time.

"There was never an attempt to put me on the sidelines. The team told me that they understood that life's circumstances had derailed me for a while and they were committed to seeing me through it," said Matt Perreault. "It's worked to everyone's benefit because today I'm back at the top of my game and other partners are benefitting from what I'm doing now. That was upside down for a few years when I was getting more than I was giving. That's what a true partnership is."

I share these stories of overcoming personal setbacks to drive

home the message that Armanino offers our team the opportunities to continuously grow and evolve both professionally and personally. By becoming a better husband and father, I became a better firm leader. By allowing others to help him when he needed it most, Matt is now able to return that compassion to his partners and staff. This is why we want everyone at Armanino to be able to bring their true, complete selves to work.

OUR SOUL SIDE

Since our founding, there has been a universal belief by Armanino's leadership team: People at their core are good. We all want to be good beings and we want to contribute. To me, this is the "Soul Side" of a business.

I've built on the empowerment concept that my dad and Tom Jones initiated and that Joe Moore continued. People are capable of doing more if given the chance, especially if there are articulated team goals. I believe that people will rally to the cause and surprise you with what they can accomplish.

I saw Armanino as a living, breathing example of the Conscious Capitalism credo: "Conscious businesses have trusting, authentic, innovative and caring cultures that make working there a source of both personal growth and professional fulfillment."

Best-selling author Pat Lencioni says, "...(P)eople in a healthy organization, beginning with the leaders, learn from one another, identify critical issues, and recover quickly from mistakes. Without politics and confusion getting in their way, they cycle through problems and rally around solutions much faster than their dysfunctional and political rivals do. Moreover, they create environments in which employees do the same."

Pat uses the word "healthy," while I refer to it as the "soul" of our business. His book, *The Advantage*, inspired our executive leadership team to come together and define the optimal state for Armanino's organizational health.

We had learned from the Berger Lewis merger that we needed greater clarity for new team members joining the firm. We were running the firm a certain way, and we had certain beliefs. But we hadn't put words to this approach. We hadn't formalized it. We tried to express who we strove to be through the Jeff Soulages Values Award, but with each year that passed since Jeff was with us, more and more people joined the firm who didn't have a personal connection to his legacy.

Figuring out our smart and soul sides of the business was the launching point to a more modern, effective way of communicating our values. We recognized that a handful of leaders could have a huge impact on the firm by demonstrating these values in our actions and recognizing every team member who exhibited them in their day-to-day work.

In the words of former Harvard Business School professor Clayton M. Christensen, "Culture, in compelling but unspoken ways, dictates the proven, acceptable methods by which members of the group address recurrent problems. And culture defines the priority given to different types of problems. It can be a powerful management tool."

In the first step of our process to better define who Armanino is, our Executive Committee read *The Advantage*. Then we worked with Pat Lencioni's Table Group during a two-day session that guided us to define our Purpose, Values and Anchors.

The overriding question we wrestled with was: "How do we empower our people from a client service and a personal development standpoint?"

According to Pat's writings, an organization's purpose is the reason it exists. "Employees in every organization, and at every level, need to know that at the heart of what they do lies something grand and aspirational."

Our leadership team has never failed to be aspirational, so it didn't take long to agree upon Armanino's purpose: "To be the most innovative and entrepreneurial firm that makes a positive impact on the lives of our clients and our people."

"I think we got our purpose right – having a positive impact," said Scott Copeland. "The money, pride and ego of success are great, but over time, those wear off. We're impacting a lot of people in a positive way and that's what keeps us motivated."

When it came to our "Core Values," the Table Group asked us to identify a short list of behaviors that were natural at the firm. They wanted to hear about the things that hadn't changed over time and were at the heart of our differentiation in the professional service industry. When they asked us to identify employees in the organization who embodied what was best about Armanino, our values and their definitions fell into place:

Firm First – putting the firm's interest ahead of any department or individual
Empowered – following one's passions with the freedom and support to succeed
Positive Energy – exhibiting an optimistic spirit that is a force multiplier for good across the firm
Wickedly Smart – challenging oneself to innovate, improve, and move the firm forward

"Our shared values and beliefs guide people's discretionary actions and are aligned with what we're trying to accomplish," said my brother Matt. "That's a positive culture. The soul of our organization is incredibly collaborative, compassionate, team based, and client focused."

The final exercise that energized our leadership group was to define our "Anchors." These were the beacons for our strategic decision making. They would give us clarity to overcome distractions, to stay true to our reason for existence, and to be able to say no when an opportunity that didn't fit our strategy seemed too good to turn down. We decided our three Anchors were: "Innovation, Entrepreneurialism, and Growth." From then on, every major decision for the firm would be evaluated through the lens of these three anchors.

We were excited to get the word out because we felt we'd really captured the firm's soul through this effort. But as with any great marketing campaign, whether internal or external, we took our time to develop a full launch plan for Armanino's new Purpose, Values, and Anchors. We waited for just the right moment to share them. We wanted to make sure our whole team was as enthusiastic as we were about this

path forward for Armanino.

UNITING NORTHERN AND SOUTHERN CALIFORNIA

In 2015, we found ourselves in an awkward, adolescent stage as a firm. We were large enough to attract clients from all over, but we weren't perceived as one of the top tier national firms. We knew we needed to be in Southern California.

We conducted a market analysis and identified a handful of firms in Los Angeles large enough to create a significant presence with our next merger. That exercise showed the growth in strategic leadership at Armanino. Prior to this, my dad, Joe, and I did every other acquisition by feel. If it felt like the right answer, we'd move forward. By the time we got to our Southern California expansion plan, we knew the region's players and who we wanted to target.

One of those firms was RBZ. Their CEO John Schweisberger had developed a relationship with me after hearing me speak at a conference. John and I strategized to introduce the concept of a merger by having me serve as a keynote speaker at the RBZ partner retreat. I was supposed to speak for a couple of hours, but the RBZ partners became very engaged, and they asked me to stay with them for the whole day. As I finished my comments to the group, I made an open invitation to consider joining our firms together.

"RBZ believed in the empowerment of people. We were mesmerized by Andy's message at our retreat," said retired partner Harvey Bookstein. "What we liked about Armanino is that the firm focused on bringing in people who were talented and could succeed, just like RBZ. Our vision with our merger transaction was to give young staff more opportunities and knowledge, to help them become more valuable to their clients, and to give them a chance for a better future."

"One of my favorite memories was sitting side by side with Andy and having dinner during our retreat," said partner Ken Coelho, who

led the RBZ Business Management team at the time. "It was so real, so honest. We shared a vision and had common goals.

"Armanino is always prepared to take advantage of strategic opportunities when they present themselves. Our merger was one of those instances," said Ken Coelho.

Having learned from our integration missteps with Berger Lewis, we did our best to ensure a smooth transition with RBZ. This deal was so important – no other firm outside the Big 4 had successfully connected the power of Northern and Southern California firms before. In addition to the big welcome event for the entire RBZ firm, our executive leadership team made a six-month commitment to be onsite in Los Angeles and address any concerns they had as quickly as possible. We rented a nearby apartment, and our COO Matt Armanino, our new corporate counsel Chris Carlberg, our CFO Chris Siegfried, and I each flew down on a rotating schedule for one week each month to ensure full executive coverage. Additionally, operations team members like Cathy Harrington Wilkinson, recruiter Kevin Turco and several different IT team members would travel to the Los Angeles office whenever necessary to bring stability and enthusiasm to our newest employees and partners.

"Armanino was very caring about our staff and partners during the integration process. That's the one thing that meant the most to us," said Harvey Bookstein. "If our former RBZ team members had an idea, we had an opportunity to share it with the firm. For instance, Michael Bossi brought the Caseware software to the Audit department. The firm liked it better than the current solutions in use and selected it for the future. That was empowering for all our team members to see."

Right after we did the deal with RBZ, we invited the whole firm for a team meeting at the Tech Museum of Innovation in San Jose. We unveiled our new Purpose, Values, and Anchors (the "PVAs," as they became known) in dramatic fashion.

Our combined team of 550 employees and partners walked into a ballroom, and on the back of every chair was a bright orange t-shirt emblazoned with one of our newly articulated values. No one yet knew the significance of the shirts, but people started running around the

tables to find the "Wickedly Smart" shirts and put them on! We had an equal number of shirts, but that one was by far the most popular. The meeting presentation went on to highlight certain team members who exemplified our PVAs and the cheers for each of them were thunderous. We now had a compelling tool to rally our troops around.

Pat Lencioni reinforces the power of setting the tone from the top: "When employees get the opportunity to hear their leaders talk about why the organization they joined exists, what behavioral values were used to select them during the hiring process, how the organization plans to succeed, what its top priority is...they can immediately see how they will contribute to the greater good of that organization." He likes to tell leaders that they are "Chief Reminding Officers" who can make a huge impact on their team by sincerely and continually sharing the soul of the organization.

I loved being the Chief Reminding Officer. After our launch party, "I started every meeting with our PVAs. I would give away $100 bills to the staff and managers who could recite our Purpose! Our department leaders also consistently shared the message of the PVAs – our consulting department created annual "Core Value" awards for their team to recognize those who exhibited Firm First, Wickedly Smart, Empowered and Positive Energy traits in their client work.

"I've valued 2,000 businesses in my career," said former Armanino partner Jeff Stegner. "You can tell when a CEO has a vision, and the team buys into it. Those that are successful empower their people. The leader who believes in the people has a team that stays with the firm and the good attitude spreads."

"Our secret sauce? It comes back to our PVAs. The number of people at Armanino with passion – it's huge. We are so passionate about the firm and the way we're interacting with clients and each other," said consulting partner Scott Schimberg.

We took the amazing positive energy we gained from the launch of our PVAs and set our sights on further expansion to "make a positive impact on the lives of our clients and our people."

INCREASING OUR POSITIVE IMPACT IN THE FIRM AND THE COMMUNITY

In 2015, the top initiative for our Management Advisory Board was analyzing our promotion data of female leaders in comparison to the industry. Regrettably, they found a disconnect at the firm. From first-year staff to managers and directors, we maintained a healthy 50-50 ratio of male and female teammates. Yet our partnership numbers of men and women were out of balance in comparison to Accounting & Financial Women's Alliance MOVE Project industry average of 22 percent female partners. Armanino's female partners only constituted 18 percent of the total.

As a tax director and Management Advisory Board member at the time, Min Riblett developed a presentation for our Executive Committee that outlined the opportunity for improvement. "One of the biggest lessons I've had at the firm was building the business case for the Women's Advancement Network. In front of this group of all male leaders, I spoke about how women tend not to speak up and doubt themselves when taking the next career step. I persuaded them with a story instead of just numbers."

The Executive Committee hung on every word Min shared with us that day. It was eye-opening for this group of hard-charging, risk-taking men to learn about the unspoken barriers our up-and-coming female professionals experienced. We provided unanimous support for the founding of the Women's Advancement Network in 2016 to develop an all-inclusive culture at Armanino with equal opportunities for women.

Min, along with audit partner Katerina Starkova, led the Women's Advancement Network in providing a multi-faceted campaign to increase gender diversity at the firm. They held sessions where our female partners and leaders shared their personal career paths, including the struggles and the triumphs. Partnering with our Armanino University department, they provided continuing education courses for the whole firm on unconscious bias. Finally, the team conducted internal surveys

and interviews to identify any unspoken barriers to advancement that might exist at the firm. One of those barriers was the need for women to have strong sponsorship to advance to the partnership level.

"Having somebody who advocates for you, who is a sponsor for you and your voice, is so important," said audit partner Stacie Kowalczyk, who would later become chair of the Women's Advancement Network. "When I joined the firm as a senior manager, Paul O'Grady supported me in learning from my mistakes and showed me that at Armanino, I could have a voice. I grew through those experiences and realized that Paul was informally advocating for me as I advanced to partnership."

In 2018, Armanino launched a formal Executive Access Program and a Transparency to Partnership educational track. The Executive Access Program pairs high-potential female managers with firm executive committee members to provide them with the opportunity to build relationships and drive their career advancement. The Transparency to Partnership education track is available to all team members to address any misconceptions about partner qualifications, the benefits of partnership, flexibility and expectations for partners and other relevant topics. Together, these efforts supported our firm's commitment to not only meet but eventually exceed the industry average of female partners. And Min, who I always believed in, became a success story from the program and was named an Armanino partner just a couple years after her presentation to the Executive Committee.

"I had never thought of myself, a female immigrant with English as a second language, as a partner," said Min. "Today, I feel I have made some impact in a positive way, seeing the influence I've had at the firm. The Executive Access Program filled up quickly, and we expect to see even more women taking advantage of it in the future."

Inspired by a 2016 presentation on empowerment by the Women's Advancement Network, our Director of Consulting Marketing Mary Tressel set a meeting with me. This is just one instance of hundreds where our open-door policy at Armanino has led to a powerful new initiative. Mary sat down in my office, spoke of her admiration for the firm and all the intellectually challenging assignments she'd enjoyed over the

past seven years. But she also shared her love of volunteering and told me she felt there was a pent-up desire across the firm for Armanino to do more in our communities. She pointed to the word "Foundation" that had been written on the top corner of my whiteboard for months and said, "If you ever launch an Armanino Foundation, Andy, I'd like to help you."

Up until that point, our community service and philanthropy efforts outside the Great Give were largely undisclosed. Armanino partners would make requests for the firm to donate to several nonprofit organizations during the year, but our staff was unaware of the financial contributions we were making. We also had different teams and offices participate in events like the American Heart Association's Heart Walk and holiday adopt-a-family gift drives. But none of this was coordinated or promoted firmwide. Creating a foundation was an aspiration I had for the firm for a few years. Like Mary, I believed we could do more.

After just 10 minutes of talk, I told Mary to "go for it."

Mary worked at top speed with our internal legal, audit and finance leaders to create the organization. Fortunately, Astine Alaverdyan, Armanino's assistant general counsel, had previous experience working with the Secretary of State to create a foundation. Within six months, the Armanino Foundation was up and running and accepting its first donations.

The Armanino Foundation is a testament to the deep desire our team members have for giving back to the community. Leading from the top, our partners committed to match every staff donation two for one, which has led to employee donation rates that are more than triple those of the average corporate foundation. Employees and partners are equal in nominating their favorite nonprofits for grants and we've donated hundreds of thousands of dollars each year in our local communities. Grantmaking is just part of our story.

Our approach to the Armanino Foundation reflected our persistent desire to be different. For an added "cool" factor, the Armanino Foundation launched a Volunteer Vacations program. These trips are organized by the Armanino Foundation and are community service trips

that last from 3-14 days across the U.S. and the globe. Team members get to experience the local culture while completing service projects. The first trip in June 2017 was to provide natural habitat restoration and beach cleanups for the Catalina Island Conservancy off the coast of California. Many trips followed, including rebuilding the Hurricane Harvey-damaged home of a grandmother in Houston, serving families at a free resort for Make-A-Wish families in Orlando, and even working at an animal sanctuary in Maui.

"Today's professionals are under so much strain these days, going full tilt all the time. People yearn to give back, but they don't have the bandwidth to uncover opportunities on their own," said Mary Tressel, executive director of the Armanino Foundation.

"It is about giving back to the community, of course, but it's even more about our people. The Armanino Foundation exists to empower our people, giving them multiple ways to support the organizations they and their teammates care about. We've made it easy and accessible for them to do more for others in need," said Mary Tressel.

Through the Armanino Foundation, we have uncovered multiple opportunities to create a positive impact on our community. It brings my dad's servant leadership full circle for me. Not everyone knows this, but my dad has devoted his entire retirement to service. He spends most of his time volunteering in the Santa Cruz community – supporting his church in multiple ministries and serving many times a week at a local soup kitchen.

The Women's Advancement Network and the Armanino Foundation bring our soul side together. We are opening possibilities for people to be their best selves, not only at work, but outside the firm. We encourage that because it makes them each a better person, which makes them better team members, and makes us a better organization. It's powerful.

HOW THE WEST WAS WON

The leadership team always knew we'd continue to grow in new

geographies. Dallas was the next stop – it was the number one city in the nation in terms of growth and business potential. Again, armed with market research data, we developed a list of target firms. Travis Wolff was one of the firms at the top of our list.

In the spring of 2016, my brother Matt and I attended the Harvard Executive Leadership Program, a professional development seminar custom-built for Moore Stephens North America firm partners. During the intense group projects, we gained valuable knowledge from several case studies and courses presented by world class Harvard Business School professors. Fortunately for us, we were paired up with Perry Kaufman, Travis Wolff's managing partner for the week. I already knew Perry from previous Moore Stephens North America meetings, but at Harvard, we learned that he shared a similar leadership strategy about building out a consultative practice for his firm.

"Matt and Andy shared a common vision with Travis Wolff for driving value for our clients," said Perry. "We had some of the same beliefs, but our firm didn't have the same service capabilities as Armanino. When I met them at Harvard, it seemed like Matt, Andy and I were reading off the same notes."

Shortly after the Harvard session, Perry invited my brother Matt and me to make a presentation to his partners. This merger moved fast! Travis Wolff was going through some succession challenges as their founders retired. Armanino was a good solution that provided a very clear framework for bringing the remaining partners together. They liked our training programs and our marketing machine and felt their staff would truly benefit from the merger. Armanino represented a path forward for this firm in transition.

"When we are given a strategic opportunity like a merger, the answer is never 'No.' It's always 'Yes,'" said audit partner Matt Perreault. "Every other firm is so risk-averse. Our focus is on how will we make it happen?"

It's a strength and compliment for our firm to be so focused on the benefits for our merger partners. At Armanino, it's very real to make the positive happen. Most accounting firms are paralyzed by the negative,

and people in our industry tend to talk themselves out of opportunities.

"We spend a lot of time to get aligned around cultural fit and sharing our vision of the future. We make sure the merging firms want to go there, too," said current COO and partner Chris Carlberg. "I suspect that other firms spend more time on economic filters of the transaction. That effort we put in at the start on culture and future view is well worth it."

We launched this merger transaction with a great slogan from our AMF Media Group division: "How the West Was Won." I wore cowboy boots to the announcement event, and we took an extensive group of partners, managers and staff from our Northern California, Southern California, and Chicago offices to meet our new colleagues. By the time the merger officially took place on January 1, 2017, our entire team was excited about the growth possibilities in Dallas.

"One of my favorite memories at the firm was the announcement of our merger," said Perry. "I was passionate about what we could do for our clients as a combined firm. We brought people out from a variety of offices and demonstrated our integration on that announcement day. It was a great signal to everyone that people really matter at Armanino."

Our dual focus on the smart and soul sides of our business is what makes our inorganic growth strategy so successful.

"When we merge in another firm, we do the right thing," said our CFO Chris Siegfried. "I value the people I've gotten to know through these transactions, I've been a safe sounding board for the onboarding partners. Our North Star is to do the right thing for the people and for the firm."

RECREATING THE DEPTH CHART

Over the next several months, Matt and I worked diligently on a new project – CEO succession. Fifteen years of the same voice is a long time for any organization and Armanino was ready for a new voice, a new perspective to continuously shape the firm to meet the challenges of the future. My long-standing belief in empowering young leaders and in being firm first made it easy to see this was the right decision

for the whole team.

I believe a leader has a couple of important jobs: to be inspiring and to get the firm ready for when you're not there. I recognized that the time was right for Armanino to have a new leader to help our firm continue to grow and transform. Armanino's past success represented by my leadership should not be an impediment to new and different ideas that will lead to future growth and success. And just as I knew exactly who I wanted for my first COO, I knew the best candidate for our next CEO was my brother Matt.

This time, I didn't have to ask him twice. He was so ingrained in all the growth we had achieved since 2008, in every merger transaction and strategic decision. He was on fire to lead the firm just as I had been in 2005.

"A highlight of my time with Armanino was the time I spent working with Andy," said my brother Matt. "We are the best of friends, but we had never before shared an overlap of work relationships. What a wonderful experience! I appreciate the value he brought. I could share my skillset and partner with him, and we accomplished things together we couldn't have done alone. We complemented each other and we able to build something together that others care deeply about."

When we publicly announced our leadership transition on March 1, 2018, many in the industry and the firm were surprised. Touchingly, a lot of people asked about my health. I didn't have any personal health issues that forced the decision. But I knew the health of the firm depended on executing this succession plan with the same professionalism that had always allowed Armanino to continue to evolve. As the months went by, everyone recognized that the firm wasn't going to miss a beat with Matt now in the driver's seat.

"Armanino has been able to recreate the depth chart decade after decade," said industry advisor Allan Koltin. "The industry asked, 'Can Armanino keep it going after Andy retires?' Matt has a different style, but it works. I see Armanino as one of the next billion-dollar firms. But it's never been about chasing a number for Armanino. It's been about their core values."

Armanino has kept going and growing and I'm so proud of it. We've

created this environment where our team gets the learning they want, the challenges they want. They are empowered and they will drive our continued growth.

"Our shared values and beliefs are no accident," said Matt. "They are a pretty simple formula that will get us to the future. We care about the team more than the individual. It is a gift from our founders and key leaders that gives us a guidepost for our future success."

BUILDING THE ARMANINO ARMY THROUGH BALANCE

As I worked year after year to build the best firm in the industry, I knew true success for the firm meant a balance between the smart and soul sides of the firm. While "do the right thing" worked as a mantra for my dad, Tom Jones, and Joe Moore when Armanino was a small organization, it wasn't enough as we grew. As leadership expands, you can try to instill that ethic through the ranks, but the interpretation of "the right thing" for one person can be different than it is for another. What people are willing to compromise on in order to get to the right thing becomes different. Soon, you're not on the same page as an organization.

"If you want to hold together a culture, you need to lay out what knits you together. You need to be clear about it," said former Berger Lewis partner and retired Armanino partner Larry Kuechler. "Values can atrophy – there are plenty of currents that could drive us in different directions. I think Armanino is special because we are constantly reaffirming the values that are here and keeping them front and center."

By running a successful firm on the smart side, I was allowed the freedom to focus on our soul side and expand the positive impact of the things that were innate in the firm from the start. In marketing our PVAs internally, we've been able to get people to not only rally to the cause but to embody it.

"Our core values are incredibly important. They are the pillars upon which we've grown from San Leandro to where we are today," said

Paul O'Grady.

Success isn't only measured by partner profitability. Success is measured by mentoring people and bringing people up in the organization and seeing them blossom and it's measured by positive client outcomes. We found a really good way to make money, but we found a way to do much more than that.

Armanino is built for the future because of our collective belief that we can achieve really high marks on the smart side and the soul side of the business. That allows us to also create a culture where people thrive, where people feel there is a good will in the organization, where we can accomplish great things for our clients and our communities.

"Everyone I've met at Armanino is on fire about the firm," said Mike Platt. "When I visit your firm, I see people who want to be part of the 'Armanino Army.' The firm has defined its 'why.' As a successful organization, Armanino has a responsibility to give back and is so intentional about it, it permeates their souls."

The firm's history illuminates our PVAs. We set high expectations. We expect things to work. We expect our team to strive for the best. We've morphed and changed and connected our firm structure to what we need to be successful in the future. Yet, we've maintained our strong ties to the past, our core values. I look at the firm today and see that we are special and different.

One of my favorite quotes from Former U.S. Secretary of State and four-star general Colin Powell is: "Perpetual optimism, believing in yourself, believing in your purpose, believing you will prevail, and demonstrating passion and confidence is a force multiplier. If you believe and have prepared your followers, the followers will believe."

"I think the PVAs are really important for us to be able to hang our hat on as a firm," said former Travis Wolff and current Armanino partner Perry Kaufman. "Not even the specifics of the PVAs, but the foundational principles that show how the firm makes their decisions and that these things are the important things. That's what helps bind a group together, especially a group as large as Armanino. I think the PVAs are really centered on helping others and that's what drives most

of us, even if we don't realize it. Our world – it's about people."

Our firm wanted to give people purpose. Accounting, audit, tax, and consulting – these are all good jobs. You learn a lot and you gain technical skills in this industry, but it's not what inspires people to give extra, to care more. To do that, you must give your organization purpose. And we have.

"I certainly see that the people attracted to, recruited to, and retained by Armanino have a high sense of values and belonging in the firm," said Rick Davis, managing partner of Elliot Davis. "There's a profound sense that people believe they're a part of something and they are moving forward together."

"Armanino has a deep, ingrained passion with reserves that provides it with the ability to stay the course," said Moore Global CEO Anton Colella. "A lot of firms have great leadership, but they lack passion. Armanino tells everyone at the firm: 'Do greater things beyond yourself.' Armanino is an organization with a great soul and passion."

We are a firm that allows a blossoming for people who have soul. I'm thankful for our founders who allowed us "up and comers" to blossom and be the best of what we could be. They didn't limit us. I'm most grateful for this start I had, and I've tried to give it back to others by believing in them. It is a powerful invitation for our future employees who want to join more than an accounting firm.

Dean Quiambao
Positive Energy

Dean graduated from UC Davis with a Bachelor of Science degree in Managerial Economics and only 11 accounting units under his belt. When he spoke about his first interview with Armanino, Dean said, “There was a leadership team in place that made it easy for me to buy into. You could see it and feel it. Once you got here, you were empowered to create and try things.”

Audit was Dean’s first practice area at Armanino and while there, he earned his CPA. Along the way, he considered leaving the firm, but I wouldn’t let Dean leave. So, he gave tax a six-month try, then returned to audit. Eventually, Dean had the choice to become a practice leader or forge his own path in business development. He followed his dream to build relationships for the firm and became our Chief Relationship Builder.

Dean says, “I’m a morning person. I’m high energy. The funny thing is—my morning is extremely calm, extremely mellow. I wake up before my whole household. Before I eat, I pray for everyone else who needs prayer more than I do. That really gives me a very grateful attitude and makes me realize how lucky I am to do a job I love. Armanino’s mindset and culture are that we care and we’re constantly curious. People can thrive here and I’m grateful for my opportunity to shine. I’d run through a wall for Armanino!

“There are three things that help me focus my positive energy every day. First, I have a grateful mindset. I’m very protective of my mindset. I have big things I want to do. Does that mean I have to turn off the news?

Yes! I'm a first generation American from an immigrant family. I had a lot of family members sacrifice for me to be in this position today. I want to take advantage of it.

"Second, I'm all about competition. Everyone loves *Hamilton*, right? I love the song lyric – 'I'm not throwing away my shot.' So many people in this industry are just going through the motions. Not us, that's not Armanino. We're young, hungry, and scrappy!

"Finally, I put in the grit. Every day, I give one percent better than yesterday, and I make progress. Our leaders will tell you that innovation happens in the smallest of improvements, not in the home run. This is how we stay innovative."

Geoffrey Wayong

Wickedly Smart

Geoffrey took a long journey around the world to find Armanino. Born in Indonesia, Geoffrey traveled to Australia at age 15 to Wesley College. His next stop was the University of California, Davis, where he earned a degree in computer science and engineering. After working in industry for a medical device manufacturer and an energy company, Geoffrey found his home at the firm. Today, he is a research and development leader in Armanino's Data and Analytics group, creating products that can be delivered to clients and to all departments of the firm.

"Data reporting has always been part of my career," said Geoffrey Wayong. "At PG&E, I was responsible for processing 18 million power meters throughout California that recorded readings every 15 minutes."

Geoffrey joined Armanino in 2006 as a Microsoft Dynamics GP technical consultant. Working next to a bookshelf filled with technical handbooks, he became fluent in 20 computer languages over the course of his career. "When I first joined the workforce, there wasn't much on the Internet and no such thing as on-demand

training courses," he said. "The job couldn't wait, so the only thing I could rely on were my technical books to find the answers to the errors my clients were experiencing." In addition to his technical language proficiency, Geoffrey is also bi-lingual in Indonesian and English.

In 2008, when the recession hit Armanino's technology consulting practice, Geoffrey's development and implementation team was running short of work. He recognized that clients were trying to extend the lives of their legacy enterprise resource planning systems. Geoffrey brought the concept of business intelligence (BI) solutions and the Qlik product to Armanino.

"I thought this might be the next big thing," said Geoffrey. "Tom Mescall told me that I had to sell Qlik to a client first before we could fund a partnership with this software company. Construction was still booming at the beginning of the recession, so our first BI client was F. Rodgers, one of the largest Dynamics GP clients we had at the time.

"To launch the BI practice, my team and I had to do it all – marketing, presales and sales. The first five clients were tough to sell. Even though the Qlik software was cheaper than other options, no one wanted to spend money at that time. Tom, Matt Armanino and Andy Armanino all opened doors for us.

"Our success has a lot to do with the firm's innovative mindset. We drank our own champagne, creating a BI dashboard that pulled data from Armanino's time entry system that gave an instant picture of how we were performing as a business. Andy and Matt believed in our intellectual property so much, they shared it at the Moore Global conferences. We implemented the same system to a handful

of Moore firms and then we partnered with CCH, a global software company, to offer the dashboard to accounting firms across the nation.

"I have stayed at Armanino because I know I'm a person who's looking for something more dynamic. I need challenges, I need change going on. I value the different challenges I am offered here and the opportunity to explore different avenues to solve them. The people and the innovative culture have kept me here."

"Serving the Community Since 1866"
Yolanda
Martha's Kitchen

PEOPLE'S
CHOICE

THANK GOD IT'S
APRIL 15TH

PURPOSE

To be the most innovative and entrepreneurial firm that makes a positive impact on the lives of our clients, our people and our communities.

VALUES

How We Behave

Firm First

We support one another and always put the firm's best interests ahead of department or individual concerns.

Empowered

We encourage our people to follow their ideas and passions, and we give them the freedom to succeed.

Wickedly Smart

We never stop challenging ourselves and each other to innovate, improve and move the firm forward.

Positive Energy

Our positive attitude and spirit is the force mutliplier that drives our success.

Courageously Connected

We embrace a diverse connected community where all belong. Unmuted as their unique authentic self, everyone is valued and celebrated.

PURPOSE VALUE ANCHORS

ANCHORS

How We Succeed

Innovation

We are trailblazers and idea generators. We embrace change and are not afraid to take risks in order to serve our clients better.

Entrepreneurialism

We empower our people to share new ideas and help them build upon those ideas within the firm.

Growth

We help our clients grow, we pursue profitable growth for the firm, and we help our people grow. We create opportunities for them and give them the tools and support to succeed.

WOMEN'S
ADVANCEMENT
NETWORK
Promoting Opportunities for Women in Executive Roles

armanino

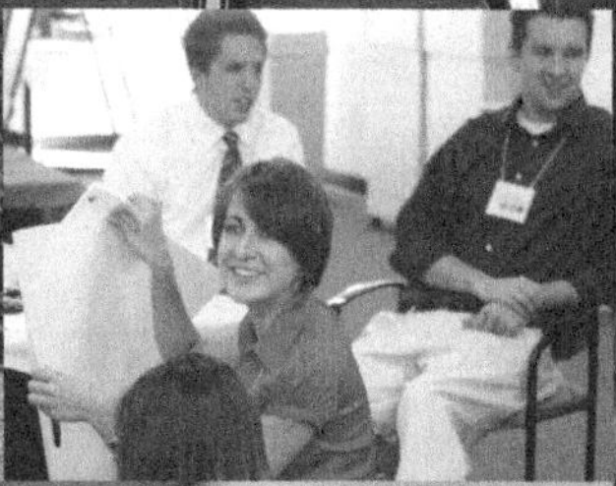

armani
anino

CAT

04

Our Finest Moment

2019-2021 | By Matt Armanino

> "Armanino has energy and compassion all driving towards one result–the firm. We recognize that it's not all figured out and we're still working on it, but Armanino has retained a sense of collaboration and family as a big firm."
>
> \- Dave Hirsch, Partner

Two years before I became Armanino's CEO, the firm introduced a powerful concept to our clients and our internal team through our annual CFO Evolution education series. The concept was "VUCA" – the acronym for Volatility, Uncertainty, Complexity and Ambiguity. It was first introduced by the U.S. Army War College to describe the multilateral world resulting from the end of the Cold War. By 2017, Harvard Business School had adopted VUCA to describe the ever-shifting business landscape. Forces like disruptive business models, the Fourth Industrial Revolution, unpredictable geopolitical shifts, and global climate change were constantly impacting our clients and our own industry. We surveyed our CFO clients, and they told us they believed that those who failed to transform their business models in response to VUCA faced existential threats.

For Armanino, I felt this was a call to action. The key to our future success lay in how agile we would be in responding to VUCA. The ultimate measuring stick of our success would be whether our own internal pace of change could keep up with the disruptive forces around us. In other words, those who are fast would prevail over the slow.

Edith Onderick-Harvey wrote for the Harvard Business Review: "Successful change-agile leaders at all levels in the organization respond to changes in the business environment by seizing opportunities, including throwing out old models and developing new ways of doing business. They try to make change thinking contagious, embedding it into everything they do from the most fundamental daily interactions to the most complex strategy."

Our leadership team rallied the Armanino team to meet this transformation challenge by sharing stories of the companies who found opportunity in VUCA and rose to the top of their industries – Amazon, Netflix, and Uber. We began to think about new, untested ways to deliver client value, to increase efficiencies in our operations, and to see around the corner for the next opportunity to differentiate our firm from our competitors.

We knew our best new concepts were not going to come from a small leadership group at the top of our firm. We needed ideas to pop up from everyone, from staff and managers to directors and partners. To encourage this crowdsourcing mentality, I shared with our team this allegory:

> Think of our future challenges and opportunities like a hiking trek to the top of 3,800-foot Mt. Diablo, a peak located just north of our San Ramon office. If I simply told you that we must reach the top, you might start thinking about how exhausted you would be, how many times you might stumble and end up scratched and bruised. Your enthusiasm level for participating in this expedition would be pretty low.
>
> But how might you regard the journey if I told you that once we were at the top, we'd have the most beautiful views of the entire Bay Area and a magnificent feast to share in celebration of our joint accomplishment? That is the "why" for taking the hike. And if I shared with you that we were going to get there by first collaborating to lay out the safest, fastest route and ensuring we had the supplies we needed for the journey, you would then be equipped with the "how." I believe that a lot more of you would be eager to take the hike once you were provided with these missing pieces.

Organizations that focus just on the "what" of their future goals get stuck in contractual relationships with their team members. Their employees do the bare minimum to adhere to their job duties. Instead, Armanino strives for powerful covenantal relationships with our whole team. By laying out the "why" and "how" of our future vision, we empower team members with the knowledge that we care deeply about them and their contributions. We see it in their discretionary activities, those times when our team members stretch beyond their daily obligations. When they raise their hands to share new ways of serving our clients, taking on new responsibilities, and learning, growing, and developing professionally, it is Firm First and all for the greater good of Armanino.

Returning to that acknowledgment that Armanino would achieve more by seeking input from more voices, we set some very strategic goals around internal governance to help us bridge the gap from the past 50 years of success to the next 50 years. For me, this meant broader and more inclusive leadership teams.

As I began my term as CEO in 2019, Armanino changed our internal governance structure by bringing more partners into the leadership tent and split the broad swath of our Executive Committee responsibilities into three new committees that work collaboratively. The Transformation Committee prepares the firm for the future by identifying new market offerings, technology solutions and other initiatives to keep Armanino nimble and responsive to client needs. The Board of Partners oversees a variety of firm activities, including the Partner Nominating Committee, Partnership Agreement changes, firmwide quality control initiatives and more. The Operating Committee manages the day-to-day operations of the firm, including the annual strategic plan and budget, departments, industry initiatives, regional offices, and governance.

In the past, we had centered our service delivery and growth plans on Armanino's service lines. This focus on internal things that matter only to our firm naturally narrowed our view of the world. Today, Armanino's overriding objective is to get closer to our clients by better understanding their opportunities and adding greater value to them. We expanded membership of the Operating Committee to include Matt Chavez as the partner leading the technology industry and Paul O'Grady leading the nonprofit industry, our two largest client segments. Their addition to our leadership team elevated our purview beyond Armanino's internal structure to include our client industries.

This was the first step in becoming an organization that focuses primarily on the markets we serve, and we started what will be an ongoing mindset change for Armanino. By setting expectations that we will define success on how well we are serving our key industry segments, that we will collaborate and work differently, that our team members will advance their careers differently – this was a sweeping change that set the stage for deeper and deeper industry focus for the next few years.

We believed this governance renewal improved transparency and increased leadership opportunities, augmented involvement in strategic initiatives and, most importantly, increased client-centric collaboration. Making a significant governance change in our business and more than tripling the number of partners at the helm of our firm operations was a big deal, no doubt. But the process of change is constant for Armanino. We did it because we saw an opportunity to be more successful, relevant, unique, and efficient in the marketplace. We were driven by positive motivators, by the things that were necessary to maintain the success we've experienced in the past. I'm proud of the fact that the firm made a seamless leadership transition and that the incredible culture we've created and curated hasn't changed. Our changes were evolutionary, not revolutionary.

"Our governance modifications were indicative of the firm's willingness to take something that was operating really well and make it even better," said partner and COO Chris Carlberg. "It was really important to broaden the number of people in leadership – it gave voice to our future-oriented younger partners. They now have a say in how the firm evolves."

ENTRY INTO NEW, UNTESTED SERVICE LINES

Armanino was poised for incredible growth and experimentation in 2019 with a passion to help our clients address the multitude of opportunities and challenges swirling around them. We started by introducing strategy, assurance, and systems implementation services to the blockchain industry, something no other leading accounting firm offered. And in true Armanino style, the concept for this groundbreaking service offering came from two up-and-coming managers in our Risk Assurance and Advisory Services (RAAS) practice, Noah Buxton and Jeremy Nau. Blockchain is an open, distributed ledger technology that can record transactions between two parties in an efficient, verifiable, and permanent way. Our client Coinbase is a blockchain exchange operator and to prepare for their complex audit, Noah and Jeremy built a makeshift "blockchain lab" in one of our small conference rooms, exploring their self-proclaimed "totally nerdy interest" in the industry.

"We knew we were going to be working with the smartest people in crypto, so we wanted to be prepared to ask the right questions and get comfortable with ways to test their balance sheets," said Jeremy Nau.

Their next step was to make a presentation to the firm's Operating Committee about the market opportunities in blockchain for Armanino.

"In hindsight, I was a little naïve," said Noah Buxton, now a partner with the firm. "I thought this could become a specialized service line with our RAAS practice, but the Operating Committee came back with the idea to make it a separate practice."

From our leadership team's perspective, blockchain technology and crypto assets had the potential to become a high impact innovation bringing value and security to businesses. We provided the operational structure and support to allow the blockchain team to incubate this concept into a full-fledged service and product offering. By October 2019, the blockchain practice had launched the TrustExplorer product, achieving an industry milestone as the world's first application of real-time attestation. For years, thought leaders had predicted the future arrival of real-time auditing capabilities and Armanino had accomplished this theorized innovation. The first license to Armanino's TrustExplorer platform was granted to TrustToken, the world's fourth largest stablecoin issuer. As of this writing, TrustExplorer is utilized by industry leaders as a crypto-focused transparency tool and has over $28 billion in assets under Real-Time Attest.

"Auditing has always relied on looking backward at historical information so that any report one is looking at is already out of date," said Scott Copeland, audit partner at Armanino. "By moving beyond time-intensive traditional methods to tools that provide instant feedback with real-time information, auditors are empowered to not just provide an opinion on past events, but to help clients make strategic decisions about the future of their finance organizations."

Another area where the accounting profession had been hesitant to engage with clients was the cannabis industry. Before we launched our own cannabis practice, Armanino sought the insight of a corporate ethicist and worked with our legal team to develop a framework to evaluate the legitimacy of potential clients. That framework includes background checks on key executives and annual reviews and ongoing determinations to ensure the cannabis clients we work with are in full compliance with the laws of every state in which they operate.

Once these prudent measures were in place in April 2019, we became one of only a few accounting firms to enter the market and provide services to clients from all sectors of the industry. We saw a great opportunity to fill a gap in the market with specialized expertise for this emerging industry.

"The cannabis industry was starving for reputable accounting and consulting firms to work with," said Ken Teasdale, Armanino audit partner and one of the Cannabis practice leaders. "Armanino provides a variety of compliance, technology and strategy solutions to help them optimize their operations and mitigate certain risks as the legitimate industry matures. We give our clients unmatched peace of mind as they scale their businesses to meet demand."

In November 2019, we added state and local tax expert Mike Goral to our cannabis industry leadership team. An industry expert, Mike was a contributing editor for the "Cannabis Taxation" treatise for Thompson Reuters. His enthusiasm to build Armanino's cannabis practice is infectious and the leadership team which includes consulting partner Jeremy Sucharski continues to mature and expand as legalization of adult cannabis use expands across the U.S. The practice grew exponentially from a half million dollars in revenues in 2019 to $3.6 million in 2020.

One of the VUCA challenges facing all companies was how to manage and make business decisions from the data they were drowning in. Research showed that 75 percent of companies believed that Artificial Intelligence (AI) was fundamental to their future success, but the majority weren't taking advantage of the AI technology available because they didn't know how to use it.

The Armanino AI Lab was launched in May 2019 to serve as a one-stop shop for its members to harness the opportunities that AI offered without being left behind by their competitors. Our practical approach to integrating AI in day-to-day working environments focused best practice usage of three core components of AI: predictive analytics, robotic process automation and virtual assistants.

Prior to launching our AI Lab, Armanino spent months researching the most common business cases for utilizing AI across the enterprise from finance, supply chain, customer experience and talent management to compliance and privacy. By developing this business case research, the Armanino AI Lab provided members with access to ready-to-deploy, proof-of-concept AI models that could be modified and customized to their specific organizational needs.

"The Armanino AI Lab presented a unique opportunity for organizations to collaborate, understand and ultimately deploy practical AI business solutions," said Matthew Pingatore, CEO of Packet Fusion. "I was excited to be a part of the founding group of members and looked forward to what we could accomplish together."

"Armanino has an identity – that identity is innovation," said Tom Rosenbach. "Firms like mine have certainly benefited from having Armanino in the Moore Global network. It gives you that confidence to try something new when you see Armanino launching innovative products and services."

EXPANDING OUR TAX EXPERTISE AND GEOGRAPHIC FOOTPRINT

While we love cultivating brand new practice areas at Armanino, we never lose sight of the core of our business. The audit, consulting, and tax services we provide are critical for the day-to-day operations of our clients. When you look at the incredible complexity and ever-changing nature of tax law, it's easy to see that our tax team is part of the bedrock of this firm. It's a juggernaut that's so important to our clients.

As we ended 2018 and entered the new year, we established a national tax office to ensure our clients had the specialty expertise they needed. Before making this move, Armanino had looked at other firms' national office models and we didn't like what we saw. These other groups set their national tax experts apart, allowing them to be aloof and indifferent to the practical needs of their clients.

Not surprisingly, we sought to be different. Armanino called our national tax team "NOW," in deliberate reference to how quickly this team would respond and help our client service teams deliver answers for our clients' new and vexing tax issues.

Armanino's NOW team is a group of experts embedded in the firmwide practice to bring more value to our clients. They provide insights on complex tax challenges such as reporting related to provision, compensation and benefits, international tax, state and local tax, research tax credits and transfer pricing. Each NOW team member provides thought leadership not just to our team members, but to our clients and prospects, sharing their domain expertise on the latest compliance requirements and tax law developments.

We also placed bets on geographic expansion in burgeoning markets throughout the West. In March, we opened our full-service foothold in Seattle, providing audit, tax, and consulting services to a variety of technology clients.

"I have found that I'm a much better fit for a growth-oriented firm like Armanino. I envisioned building Armanino's Seattle/Pacific Northwest practice two years before I exited EY," said partner Doug Sirotta. "The personality of the firm is that we are a can do and action firm. We have energy for market-facing growth.

"I've had the best of both worlds. I spent almost 27 years working in mid-size or Big 4 firms that were great and had a lot of infrastructure. But there was a downside to that, too. There was so much politics and infrastructure that it inhibited growth. Armanino doesn't have encumbrances. We're very open. I like not having barriers to grow," said Doug Sirotta.

Armanino had been strategically investing to ensure we could better serve the Los Angeles area with an expanded geographic footprint that covers all the major hubs in the region. We were so impressed with the Bolar Hirsch & Jennings team and they saw us as a path to the future for their team. With this addition, we had a total of five offices throughout Southern California.

"I'm a do-it-yourself guy – we had our own firm for 30 years. But we started asking ourselves, 'Where is our firm going next?'" said former Bolar, Hirsch & Jennings name partner and current Armanino partner Dave Hirsch. "We talked to a lot of firms in our search for one that had the same values as us and offered greater opportunities for our people.

"We saw Armanino as highly entrepreneurial, collaborative, caring about their people, and humble about what they did well and what they were working on to improve. I wanted to find a great place for our people, where they would be respected, appreciated, and pushed to excel. I'm seeing our people thrive. Virtually all our clients have stayed. It's been a really good experience," said Dave Hirsch.

Armanino's leadership team has always believed that to deliver upon a strategic inorganic growth strategy, you have to execute on a strong organic growth strategy. If you can't write your own success story, inorganic growth is false gold. We create our own success and see inorganic growth as a way to accelerate things we're excited about.

"A lot of mergers and acquisitions in our industry occur when one of the firms can't make the transition between generations or haven't invested for the future," said partner and COO Chris Carlberg. "Armanino is unique in our ability to attract thriving firms that want to join forces with us. Not because they need to merge, but because they see we can accelerate each other down a shared path of success."

"Our mergers are one plus one equals three. We are not buying revenue – that's boring and easy. Everything is about opportunity. Then, we fold in the power of Armanino," said partner Ken Teasdale.

Throughout our firm history, there were many other great people and firms who joined us through business combinations. Armanino got stronger each and every step of the way with the addition of new teams and areas of expertise. For a comprehensive list of the firm's business combinations, please see the addendum.

The next stop for Armanino's geographic expansion was Denver in July. Our tax leader David Sordello had been cultivating a relationship with Chris Becze, who had an impressive reputation as the strategy and growth partner for TaxOps, a local Denver firm. David shared his success with risk-taking at Armanino with Chris, just as he does with all new tax leaders who join the firm.

"This is a place where you can do your own thing in your own way," said David Sordello. "There's support and structure, but the firm also trusts people enough to empower them to do their own thing. If you're successful at that, it compounds and grows. The entrepreneurial spirit is what kept me here."

"Armanino is a group of professionals that are all moving forward, and hell bent on it," said partner Chris Becze. "It's so intoxicating—here the sky's the limit. I wanted to be a part of Armanino. Within a year of opening the office, we acquired a lot of good clients. It's fulfilling, exciting. I've always had a growth mindset and I felt like I was handed the keys to the kingdom when I arrived at the firm."

Of course, I'd spoken with Chris Becze during our negotiations for him to lead our Denver office, but I didn't realize what a sense of humor this former Persian Gulf Navy veteran had. I arrived in Denver in advance of our office open house event for clients and prospects. After I had greeted the new Armanino team and told them how excited I was for Armanino to be entering in this new market, Chris had a surprise for me. He handed me a box with a custom-made suit to wear to the event that evening. This wasn't just any suit – it was pale grey with the orange and green Armanino logo stamped all over the jacket and the pants!

"My favorite memory was all about getting Matt to dress up in the Armanino suit," said Chris Becze. "I still have clients who talk to me about my CEO and that suit. This is not a normal firm – the way Matt played it off was a great indicator of our company as a whole. What other CEO would do that?"

I haven't worn the suit again, but I'm glad it made such a great impression in our new market.

INTRODUCING A TRANSFORMATIVE APPROACH TO DEVELOPING OUR TEAM

In keeping with our approach to building a top-notch Operations team, we spent months seeking the right candidate for a Chief People Officer at Armanino. Armanino sought to invest in talent development and analyze how we train, assess, and build the most advanced team of professionals in the industry. One candidate rose to the top of our list because she came with a comprehensive agenda to identify the potential skillsets required to confidently guide our clients into an uncertain future.

"I was enamored when I arrived at Armanino because I didn't have to convince people that what I wanted to achieve was important," said Chief People Officer Carol Ann Nash. "We are all committed to empowering our team to serve as nimble, agile problem solvers for their clients and to stretch themselves professionally."

Carol Ann Nash's vision included a career lifecycle view, from recruiting to succession planning, that would drive aspirational career growth for all our team members. Included in that viewpoint was addressing a key shortcoming in our industry and our firm. The accounting industry is renowned for its lack of diversity – according to a 2019 AICPA blog post, "total minority hiring by U.S. CPA firms has remained flat since 2012."

As CPO, Carol Ann Nash co-leads the firm's IDEAL (Inclusion of Diverse Employees and Leaders) Team with our General Counsel Sarah Harris. This group creates actionable policies and programs that include open and honest dialogue to address disparities within our workforce. Diversity and inclusion are personal for me. It's important that people know where I stand as a leader and as a person, which is why I hold myself responsible as a signatory to the CEO Action Pledge for Diversity and Inclusion.

We try to run our business for the best results, the best outcomes. There is clear, empirical evidence that diverse and inclusive organizations are more profitable and more likely to achieve long-term growth within their industries. We need to have enough vulnerable trust to take advantage of cognitive diversity, different perspectives, unique ideas. When Armanino garners the greatest array of thought, we achieve the business imperative we seek.

"When it comes to empowerment, you want everyone to feel like they can share their ideas," said Sarah. "The power of diverse thinking will get the client the best solutions. It's important to make people feel they can speak up and bring their whole selves to work. That is the objective of Armanino's IDEAL Team."

"Being more inclusive helps you to be more competitive," said Erby Foster, CFOO of the Glide Foundation and Armanino client who addressed our team for Black History Month in 2021. "You show up better and stronger than anyone else and can leverage your diversity, equity and inclusion initiatives for a deeper connection with your clients."

How we think about recruiting talent, reskilling our people, seeking to achieve fairness by recognizing unconscious bias – this is the positive role business can play in our society. We can make changes to help the world become a fairer place and I want Armanino to lead the change in our industry.

VUCA LIKE THE MODERN WORLD HAS NEVER SEEN

We entered 2020 with a tremendous amount of momentum. We experienced 16 percent year- over-year growth in 2019 and had a long list of strategic mandates laid out for our team of 1,400 staff and partners. Our annual strategic plan aligned with the five tenets that support Armanino's aspiration to be our clients' most trusted and valued partner in an uncertain world: Maintain Client Focus, Create Differentiated Value, Keep Stride with the Pace of Change, Harness Technology and Collaborate.

Our client-facing leaders and operations team members dove into these objectives in the first quarter and our financial results in January and February saw us outperforming our budget. The stage was set for another exceptional year for the firm.

When Armanino presented our point of view about VUCA and the CFO Evolution from 2017 to 2019, I'll admit that some days, it felt like a bit of an academic exercise. Despite all the examples of disruptive business models, if a client's industry was unaffected at the time, it was easy for them to ignore the message. And I never wanted Armanino to fall into complacency, allowing our past success to limit our future accomplishments. To provide a sense of urgency to our team and our clients, I used quotes like the one from author and famed CEO Jack Welch: "If the rate of change on the outside exceeds the rate of change on the inside, the end is near."

When the COVID-19 pandemic and resulting economic crisis hit the globe, it wasn't necessary to provide a sense of urgency. It created a lot of fear, uncertainty, and complexity for how our clients' businesses and our own firm would survive this exceptional crisis. For all the unknowns swirling around us, I knew that Armanino would stay committed to the guiding principles our founders gave us and care more about our clients and about our people than anyone else.

Our People team sent out the first firmwide guidance about COVID-19 on February 28, eliminating large group gatherings in the office and encouraging healthy practices like handwashing and workstation sanitizing. Following local health official guidelines, our offices shut down, one by one. First, Seattle on March 5, then San Jose on March 13, with San Ramon and San Francisco quickly following. By March 25, all California offices, plus Seattle, Dallas, and Boise, had limited access to essential operations team members only and all other 1,400 Armanino employees across the nation were encouraged to work from home.

For those readers who've never worked in an accounting firm, the complexity created by a work-from-home environment amid tax and audit busy season was massive. Auditors customarily spend the spring traveling from client to client, road warriors providing onsite assurance services to our corporate clients. Tax team members routinely spend long days, evenings, and weekends at the office, working from three computer screens to provide maximum efficiency in processing our clients' tax returns. These teams build camaraderie around the long hours spent together delivering the highest client service. Suddenly, nothing was "normal," and our teammates were relegated to their homes, many setting up home office spaces for the first time in their careers.

Our People organization and IT team sprang into action, ensuring all the employees had the equipment and best practices guidance they needed to continue their day-to-day operations. I felt the strength of our top-flight Operations team really shine in this crisis.

"We were so successful in supporting our colleagues because of the very hard work done prior to COVID-19 by all IT team members," said Armanino CIO Gary Baumgartner. "We had a good vision, plan and projects worked on earlier that better enabled a fully mobile workforce with strong business continuity capabilities."

All around us, economic indicators painted a terrifying picture. Between February 12 and March 23, the Dow lost 37 percent of its value. Ridership on the Bay Area Rapid Transit system dropped by 25 percent in early March and by 94 percent by the end of April. "The scope and speed of this downturn are without modern precedent, significantly worse than any recession since World War II," said Federal Reserve Chair Jerome Powell on March 13.

As the month of March wound down, our Operating Committee and our finance team spent long days creating forecast scenarios, analyzing best case to worst case outcomes for Armanino. We recognized that some of our clients would not be able to pay their bills. Field work for audit was pushed out. The IRS extended the April 15 tax deadline to July 15, 2020, delaying a huge seasonal revenue stream for the firm. We took into consideration that our consulting revenues took a huge hit in the 2008-2009 Recession and we had to prepare for a similar loss of business again.

On April 7, I shared with the whole firm the several measures we'd taken to reduce costs that were unseen by the staff. We reduced partner draws, the monthly method of payment for our partners, on a sliding scale by as much as 30-40 percent for all partners. Certain partners chose to reduce those draw payments even further and some partners, including me, reduced our payments to zero. We suspended spending on all non-critical items across the firm, eliminated business travel, set a hiring freeze, eliminated temporary workers, and deferred payments on rent and to retired partners.

Now came the hardest part. I shared that even with those cuts, our leadership team still had to reduce the single largest expense in our business – labor costs. That meant a reduction of workforce by eight percent effective immediately, which we accomplished by the elimination of some positions and furloughing of others. Those reduced positions were focused in areas of our business where we had excess capacity.

We reassured our remaining team members that we had retained the people we thought would give us not only the very best chance at getting through this crisis but also at bouncing back from it. We also implemented two additional temporary changes – reducing the schedules of some Operations employees and, for the rest of the workforce, putting into place a 10 percent reduction of base compensation.

In my video address to the firm, I strove to make clear that our ultimate goal was to get the firm through this crisis, to protect as many of our team members as possible, and then to get back on our path to prosperity…the growth that we saw before this crisis. But unfortunately, I didn't really know how long "temporary" was going to last and I was honest with the team about that, too.

I ended my address by saying that because of the COVID crisis, there were a lot of things that had been put on hold or cancelled in our lives. But resiliency was not one of them. I believed in the resiliency of our firm and all the people listening.

This was the hardest day of my career. We thought we might be in ruin. We thought Armanino might not exist. I was so concerned about the impact of our decisions on our people and the pressure on them from working from home. I was concerned about whether I was the right leader for this moment and, I admit, I prayed on this. What got me through as Armanino's CEO were the countless messages of support I received from our partners and team members. They asked me how they could help, what more could they do.

A pragmatic yet touching example of this encouragement came the very next week from Barbara Carberry, our San Francisco and Seattle office administrator. She posted the following message on our intranet: "I was wondering how I personally can help the firm during this 'temporary normal.' Here's a really easy way – not submitting for my $50 monthly cell phone reimbursement. How about it? While this might not be viable for everyone, for those who can swing it, want to join me in the good deed? We're all in this together."

Her simple message became one of the most popular ever posted – 53 teammates immediately wrote back to say they were "all in" with Barbara. These individuals probably thought this was a small personal gesture, but their collaboration in support of our cost-cutting measures was so powerful to our leadership team. It was a vivid example of the covenantal relationship they had with Armanino.

STRENGTH THROUGH TOGETHERNESS AND COLLECTIVE CREATIVITY

It would be logical to expect the firm to slow down, to put our strategic plans on hold, to just move from day to day. But in this moment of crisis, the best qualities of Armanino's spirit manifested itself in our teams getting closer, our people caring more for each other, and all of us focusing more on our clients. To buoy that spirit, we created a Rallying Cry for the firm: "Strength through Togetherness and Collective Creativity." We encouraged our team to accomplish this through increased outreach to our clients and each other, an acute focus on what mattered most and the freedom to do things differently and quickly.

Our service delivery leaders, brand and field support team members coalesced into a Rapid Response Team to deliver on our Rallying Cry. They met three days a week to prioritize and provide educational resources to help our clients navigate through this crisis. The lightning speed with which this group was created and provided valuable content externally was so impressive. In all, this team produced more than 100 articles, blog entries and webinars to keep our clients aware of how the Coronavirus Aid, Relief, and Economic Security (CARES) Act and Paycheck Protection Program (PPP) impacted their businesses. In distributing this valuable content to our clients, we delivered on one of our strategic goals for the year – to collaborate across the Firm to maximize client value and differentiate Armanino in the marketplace.

"I've felt the smart side and the soul side of Armanino's approach to business in your response to the pandemic. We were receiving emails from our bankers and our attorneys, too, but Armanino shone as the smartest," said Paul Bongiovanni, Oakland Diocese CFO and long-time Armanino client. "On the soul side, I knew your people cared. When we were applying for the PPP and it meant a $1.5 million loan for our schools, (Armanino's consultant) Karen Thompson did all the paperwork overnight. She dropped what she was doing to ensure we met the deadline because she knew what was at stake. That was the embodiment of the soul side of your business."

In early April, COVID-19 was ravaging New York and hospitals were stretched beyond capacity. The New York State Department of Health needed a way to rapidly deploy antibody testing to clear healthcare professionals to get back to work on the front lines. When our technology partner Microsoft called for volunteers, Armanino's technology consultants jumped at the chance to help save lives. They worked non-stop for five days to build and create a testing tracking app for hospitals and medical centers to use. In its first week, the app provided 500 healthcare workers and their hospitals vital insight into when they could return to work. With this pro bono effort valued at $100,000, our team of committed professionals was very happy to make a difference during the pandemic. They made our whole firm proud of their positive impact amid this crisis.

In January 2020, we founded our Data & Analytics practice in conjunction with the AI Lab to bring the latest in digital transformation capabilities to our clients. Comprised of data scientists with backgrounds in computer science, the Data and Analytics team was poised to respond when COVID struck. Our team evaluated the disease metrics reporting landscape and recognized that there was significant public data about illnesses, test results and the impact the virus had on the economy. However, the scientific websites related to the disease did not answer key business "back to work" questions.

Our Data and Analytics team delivered a powerful tool for business reopening decision making on May 12. Armanino's COVID Recovery Tracker empowered users with a simple dashboard to track daily and multi-day trends for regional traffic patterns and COVID case counts.

"How we interpret the data can change how people look at this crisis," said Claudine Wong, KTVU News reporter in a May 21 interview with Armanino partners Tom Mescall and Dean Quiambao. "The (Armanino COVID Recovery) Tracker makes people feel better that they are making a decision that's not arbitrary. There's so much emotion in getting back to business, but you want to do it in the right way, to point to something."

"This new data visualization tool brought great insights to businesses and helped them to make specific re-opening decisions about their locations in individual counties across the nation," said Armanino partner Tom Mescall.

Through all this hard work to deliver solutions and answers to our clients, we knew that our team working from home was missing the community connections they had at the office and the strain of the COVID pandemic was immense for all of us. When it became obvious that safety protocols would eliminate our annual tradition of in-person Great Give activities, the Armanino Foundation pivoted to ensure our commitment to community service stayed intact. Our team and their family members participated in 10 different "virtual volunteer" activities, ranging from writing letters of support to healthcare workers and frontline responders to completing mental health first aid training.

"It was great that the Armanino Foundation was able to coordinate with so many nonprofits to truly make an impact for those in need," said Armanino partner Ken Coelho. "We got as much out of this as the organizations we helped. We definitely needed this."

The Armanino Foundation also found a way for the team to have some much-needed fun with its first-ever virtual auction. Staff and partners found connection from their home offices by outbidding one another for items like beef jerky gift packs, an Armanino-branded paddleboard, baking and cocktail-making baskets, and much more. Together with our partners two-for-one donation match, our team raised $70,000 that was used to provide COVID relief grants to 12 hospitals and healthcare organizations near our major offices.

May was a very busy month at the firm and our People team delivered on our strategic focus on enhancing our employee experiences firmwide. The launch of Elevate Learn, an AI-powered on-demand learning platform transformed our training programs. Armanino team members now had the opportunity to create their own professional development paths, with guidance from the system and without the constraints of in-person training sessions. This on-demand flexibility to select convenient times to increase their knowledge and skills was so vital to our team members balancing the demands of clients and family.

"I don't think there was anything more important in our 2020 Strategic Plan than the transformation of training our people," said Chief People Officer Carol Ann Nash. "Elevate Learn showed that we were able to make a lot of progress on key initiatives despite all the curveballs thrown our way by the COVID crisis."

In June, our nation was rocked by protests of the killing of George Floyd in Minneapolis, Minnesota. This public outcry became an inflection point. We as a nation asked, "How could that happen?" What it did, particularly for young people, was create the demand for change.

This moment presented me as a CEO with two options. Armanino could play it safe inside our four walls and use the age-old business approach of saying nothing about societal ills to avoid offending our clients, partners, and employees. On the other hand, there was an opportunity to exert leadership and call for all of us to be better as individuals, companies, and communities.

I wrote an open letter to our team and our clients, sharing that I felt the time had come for business to take action. That we must acknowledge that things have not been fair for African Americans – individually and systematically. We knew this is wrong and we needed to use our voice as a firm to make for a better world.

I reached out to our African American partners and, honestly, at first, they were too hurt by George Floyd's killing to speak to me. They needed time to find the words to explain their pain to me, a white male. In collaboration with our IDEAL Team, our partners Larry Hancock and Vintage Foster moderated a series of Community Conversations for the Armanino team. Along with Larry and Vintage, several Armanino team members and partners spoke honestly about George Floyd's killing and their life experiences of discrimination in the United States as immigrants, African Americans, Asian Americans, and Latinos.

We had more than 800 team members join us for the first Community Conversation in the middle of the COVID crisis – more than we'd ever had for any firmwide event. When that many people took time in their workday to come together with their colleagues and talk about this difficult topic, how can anyone say that business doesn't have a responsibility to do more?

"Our first three Community Conversations were all Armanino team members sharing personal stories from within," said Sarah Harris, an African American member of the human race, as she likes to say. "A lot of people felt really empowered by that experience. Empowerment gives you that lift to really show up at work. It requires safety, and it's our most important differentiator as a firm.

"Our leadership is legitimately behind making some change. It's actually uplifting," said Sarah.

"Our Community Conversations were the most real conversations that other companies were not having," said Jaclyn Armanino, Chair of the SAB in 2020 and daughter-in-law of Andy Armanino. "They weren't political. It was real people talking about their experiences of what's going on. I was so proud to be an employee."

"We're either going to be part of the problem or part of the solution. Staying silent and doing nothing doesn't help. I'm hopeful and encouraged just by having this conversation," said Cherri Jackson, a manager in our Dallas office. "I hope everyone leaves this conversation strengthened. Lastly, try and be the difference."

"I feel blessed to be part of a firm that shares and addresses these tough topics," said Sheri Carney, a senior consultant in our Seattle office. "It's obvious that you are interested in helping us grow not just as better employees, but better human beings."

We were all hurting. I believe the common thread was that we needed to have this conversation because we knew racism isn't right. We wanted to understand how this could be…that these are the ugly truths we're still living with. Our people were looking for some optimism, to find a path to being healthier, better. And they were looking for that, not just in their churches and their homes. They were looking for that within the constructs of our firm. And that's what makes me believe there is some responsibility for stakeholder capitalism. What's my obligation, my responsibility? If we had told everyone, "Go back to work," it would have been a missed opportunity.

WORKING OUR WAY OUT OF THE DARKNESS

The COVID-19 pandemic continued to rage across our nation and the world as we entered the second half of 2020. At Armanino, our team found strength by connecting with one another through online forums and supporting one another to deliver our very best service for our clients. Reflecting on the firm's origins, Armanino has always had a heartfelt belief that our commitment to our clients is our highest calling. If there was a silver lining to be had in 2020, it was that our core focus on our clients had once again guided us to the right place at the right time. Everything we believed over the previous 50 years became amplified because our clients never needed us more.

Just like family gatherings, weddings and graduations were cancelled on the personal front, live events for business were non-existent during the summer of 2020. Our annual CFO Evolution conference was reimagined by our Brand and Field Marketing teams to address this challenge. With a theme of "Navigating to the Next Normal," we wanted to bring a virtual conference that would offer business leaders mission-critical information and guidance on handling the ongoing disruption. Thirty of our experts provided 15 on-demand sessions with actionable insights to help our clients move through this volatile time. We had a record turnout of 500 guests in July and more than 850 additional business leaders viewed the online conference content by the end of 2020.

July also marked the launch of a comprehensive Return-to-Work solution suite for Armanino clients and prospects aimed at helping them manage workplace reopening in a strategic and safe manner. Our COVID-19 Return-to-Work App provided real-time visualization for company leaders with employee wellness monitoring, workspace scheduling and access to our COVID-19 Recovery Tracker. Armanino's HR consultants were available to help organizations update the myriad policies impacted by the global pandemic, from remote working and workplace safety to travel and CARES Act employee retention credits. Finally, our operations guidance helped businesses by addressing everything from lease renegotiation and insurance policy reviews to tax matters related to a changed work environment, company privacy policies, and more. With this full suite of offerings, Armanino sought to help our clients reduce their financial liability and ensure the integrity of their physical locations.

"When the time came to reopen, each business had a responsibility to create a work environment for returning employees that prioritized safety and protected the company through risk mitigation planning," said Jenn McCabe, Armanino Rapid Response Team member and consulting partner.

Our unwavering dedication to our clients during this difficult year led to the advancement of another one of our strategic objectives – increasing our firmwide focus on deepening and leveraging industry expertise. In 2019, our nonprofit and technology industry groups were launched and achieved incremental innovation when it came to collaboration across service lines to deliver value for our clients. The Operating Committee saw the potential for our industry groups to create sweeping change across the firm and in 2020, we added three new key industries to our list: real estate, healthcare, and the previously mentioned cannabis industry. Combined, these five industries represent two-thirds of the firm's revenues.

Each set of industry leaders developed strategic plans to improve collaboration in new business proposals, increase thought leadership, drive revenue growth and, most importantly, create "best and only" industry-specific service and product offerings that our clients couldn't get anywhere else. All five teams built out steering committees and subvertical groups to further concentrate their efforts on the business issues critical to our clients. For instance, the technology industry encompasses a multitude of specialty areas and Armanino highlighted its expertise in life sciences, healthtech, gaming, digital media, SaaS, fintech and more.

"We are perceived as industry leaders when we bring a multidisciplinary team of tax, technology consulting, audit, and more experts to our calls with life sciences companies," says life sciences subvertical leader and audit partner Rich Asiodche. "By demonstrating our deep industry knowledge, we show them we are the business partner who will help them to succeed."

Our nonprofit team excelled at producing best and only solutions throughout the year. They teamed with our Data & Analytics team for an ideation session that produced more than 20 potential product offerings. The Private School Financial Framework Toolkit provided school business officers a data-driven solution for forecasting the impact of COVID-19 on their tuition revenue, financial aid, and enrollment. We also created a robust Benchmarking for Nonprofits cloud-based platform to show our nonprofit clients how they compare to similar charitable organizations. The benchmarking software provides intuitive dashboards and visuals for profitability, sustainability, liquidity, and balance sheet operational metrics.

Armanino's real estate industry team brought real-time thought leadership to our clients hard hit by the COVID-19 crisis. We invited external real estate experts who focus on development, commercial space, interior design, and investments to participate in webinars with our partner David Erard on "Real Estate Trends in Our New Normal" and "How the New Normal Is Changing the Way Businesses Use Space."

Our cannabis and healthcare teams also made strides in collaborating across service lines to provide a broad set of solutions to their clients. What we learned from this year of focusing our efforts by industry vertical is that our firm has an unbelievable depth of enthusiasm, skills, intellectual property, and solutions that are just what our clients need. The more we invest time and product development to our industry groups, the more relevant we will become to our clients.

In September, we were so happy to bring our entire workforce back to full pay and full schedules. We were able to hit this milestone based on everyone's extraordinary hard work and covenantal actions. It was a cause for celebration, and we recognized that it would not have been possible without the positive energy and firm first attitude of our whole team. Our partners sent a gift box to every employee that included stress relief desk accessories and cookies as a small token of our deep thanks. The way we teamed together is what makes Armanino special, and it allowed us to find a silver lining during such a difficult year.

I took this occasion to tell our team that we were also mindful of the fact that there was more hard work ahead of us, and, while we wished there was a clear end in sight for the COVID-19 crisis, we weren't there yet. It had turned our year into more of a marathon than a sprint. I reassured the team that if they were struggling with working from home, the stress of homeschooling their kids or anything related to the pandemic, they were encouraged to reach out to our partners or our People team for help. We wanted to be there for anyone who needed more support.

As we moved into November, our blockchain team made another landmark move for trust and transparency in digital asset ecosystems. We collaborated to ensure that the Real-Time Attest product within the TrustExplorer suite could provide secure, reliable and verifiable attest data about TrustToken (the fourth largest stablecoin globally) to Chainlink, the world's largest oracle network.

"Our ability to provide unprecedented transparency continued to grow with TrustExplorer," said blockchain director Noah Buxton.

"While users always had access to our live dashboards and on-demand attest reports, Chainlink provided the first of what we hoped to be many different ways for users to access data in flexible ways that meet their needs directly on-chain."

As the year ended, we received external validation of our efforts to be the most innovative and entrepreneurial firm that makes a positive impact on the lives of our clients, our people, and our communities. Armanino received the 2020 CalCPA Society Public Service Award for the variety of ways we gave back to our local communities and reinforced the profession's commitment to the public through the Armanino Foundation. ClearlyRated, a leading provider of client satisfaction surveys and service quality research, awarded Armanino with a Best of Accounting certification for the sixth consecutive year and the firm's second Diamond Award. Achieving a 72 Net Promoter Score, Armanino was rated more than three times as high as the accounting industry average of 23. This was a 26 percent increase in our score over 2019 thanks to the firm's rapid response and agility around the COVID-19 pandemic's disruption to our clients.

GreatSchools, Inc., an Armanino client, told ClearlyRated, "(Armanino has a) stellar team - no matter who we engage with, the level of support is great. They don't just answer our questions but provide the information behind their answers."

The highlight of the year came during our last firmwide broadcast in mid-December. The firm had not only survived, but managed to thrive, achieving ten percent revenue growth during the toughest year in our history. Throughout the year, I never heard a single complaint from a team member about the salary and schedule cuts we made. We had endured so many challenges, so much strife at work and outside of work, but this online meeting reinforced the firm's deep commitment to treat our employees well and fairly.

I was so honored to share some amazingly good news with the team... news I could not foresee in March when the VUCA of the COVID-19 crisis hit Armanino and our clients full force. It brought me great joy to tell the whole team that we would true up their salaries before the end of the year, paying back the financial sacrifices they had made from April through August to ensure our firm's financial stability.

The words of our co-founder, Tom Jones, seem particularly relevant to describe how we made it through this most difficult of years: "This firm is like a clock. It ticks away, day after day keeping time, accurate, precise, reliable. It's beautiful on the outside, but it's the inside mechanism that works tirelessly behind the face of the clock that truly keeps it running."

I received so many heartwarming notes from staff and partners after that call. I share a few here to honor the courageous positive energy our team brought to their work daily in 2020.

"I particularly admired your unwavering stance that there would be no circumstances under which we as partners would benefit financially from the success that we have seen this year until our employees were trued up," said partner John Horner. "You won't be surprised that this was a message that I fully supported and which I passed on to my team several times this year. I believe this message gave us the credibility to continually ask our teams to go back into battle with us every day."

"There couldn't have been a better ending to this crazy year," said Angie Hill, a senior human resources manager in our Dallas office. "We thoroughly appreciate how this leadership team believes in their employees and walks the walk."

"What a nice surprise! It was a wonderful Christmas gift, and it could not have come at a better time," said Tanya Bi, business management services manager in Armanino's Los Angeles office. "I am so happy to be a part of this firm."

"The clarity in communication from our leaders means a lot," said Marie Leon, field support manager in our San Ramon office. "I've worked at other firms and heard their CEO messages, and they were never as relatable. Matt is very appreciative of his team and I feel I'm part of his team, an integral part of the firm's success, and that the work I'm doing is important. I see how the dots connect and it's what keeps me here."

"The silver lining of managing through this difficult year was the collaboration we hadn't seen before. We did a yeoman's effort to work through this year and we've come out stronger for it," said partner and COO Chris Carlberg.

LOOKING FORWARD

Armanino began 2021 with the perspective that the COVID-19 crisis would continue to be a marathon. Knowing a lot of challenges and risks still lay ahead, I chose to focus on the abundance of opportunity available to our firm. Our leadership team believed there were more ways to add value to our clients than ever before, and we developed a strategic plan to deliver on that promise.

First, we announced the internal promotion of 14 new partners, the largest class in our firm's history. Despite the challenges posed by the pandemic, Armanino continued to create opportunities for our star performers. Underscoring our efforts to provide a diverse and inclusive work environment, we were very pleased that 43 percent of the new partner class were women. The growing pipeline of women pursuing partnership was directly attributable to the efforts of the Women's Advancement Network.

Next, we held our first ever virtual Partner Rally Kickoff, creating energy around our 2021 strategic plan and our design for the future. One pillar of our Vision 2025 plan was growth and we set our sights on doubling the size of the firm to $800 million in revenues over the next five years. As our leadership team saw it, sustainable profitable growth has always been the lifeblood of our firm. It is not growth for growth's sake, but the incredibly important output of everything else we do. Armanino's growth allows us to make investments in innovation and to stoke our entrepreneurial spirit by empowering people to pursue their passions and ideas.

Investing in our people through the Elevate strategy to transform their professional development was another key element of Vision 2025. Our goal was to drive aspirational career growth with accessible training and experiences that supported everyone from new college recruits to firm veterans ready for succession planning. We sought to be the most inclusive and diverse major firm and the number one firm for stars in the industry. We put those goals into action by recruiting for the first time at historically black colleges and universities and sponsoring industry organizations like the National Association of Black Accountants, ASCEND for Pan-Asian professionals and the Association of Latino Professionals For America with grants from the Armanino Foundation. Armanino's people are our marketplace advantage and empowering them to fully realize their dreams at our firm will always be a top priority.

Brands are the core identity of any company. The accounting industry often swims in what I call a "sea of sameness." Our critical brand goal is to help Armanino continue to stand apart as the most unique firm in the industry. We will be known in the marketplace as the firm that sees the world through our clients' eyes and provides industry-specific best and only solutions to them. Building off our experiences in 2020, we also sought to galvanize our team members in providing best-in-class client experiences.

Vision 2025's final pillar was transformation. By automating 100 percent of repeatable tasks and continued investment in our data and analytics capabilities, we will increase our value to our clients. Chris Carlberg told our partners, "Our future success is tied to our ability to successfully execute on our transformation roadmap. I believe our pace of change and transformation actually needs to increase in anticipation of our client needs. We're well positioned to deliver on that with our industry focus and innovative solutions."

In March, Armanino successfully completed a rigorous assessment process to become the world's largest Certified B Corporation accounting and consulting firm. The only third-party certification that measures a company's entire social and environmental performance, B Corporation evaluated Armanino's business model and operational impact on our customers, workers, community, and the environment. It was validating to see that our firm achieved the maximum available points for all categories related to our customers and top scores for several categories focused on our team members and community service.

"This is close to my heart," said Anthony Rotolo, a strategy and transformation consultant who was a key contributor to our certification efforts. "Armanino's B Corporation certification validates our purpose and the legacy of our founders. It's a powerful statement to anyone working with us or considering joining the firm that we are using our business as a force for good."

"The B Corporation designation is one that all firm leaders can share with pride," said retired managing partner Andy Armanino. "It illustrates that all the investments we've made over the years in training and empowering our team to be better professionals and better people delivers a positive impact for our clients and our communities, too. We've created this mutually beneficial loop for all stakeholders with our balance of the smart side and the soul side of Armanino."

Achieving B Corporation certification also gave the firm the inspiration to pursue a new service offering for our clients – Environmental, Social and Governance (ESG) Advisory Services. In 2021, we saw a sea change in the measurement, reporting and creation of ESG metrics that our clients would need to address. The European Union passed strict anti-greenwashing reporting requirements for all companies doing business there in March. SEC Chairman Gary Gensler issued a call for public comment on ESG reporting requirements for public companies in the United States in the summer. And Harvard Business Journal went so far as to publish an article outlining how "accountants would save the world" through sustainability accounting.

Armanino launched our new service line because we care deeply about sustainable and equitable business practices. We seek to help our clients drive progress and build successful, resilient business models so they can thrive no matter what environmental and social challenges come their way. It was exciting to see the enthusiasm to build this new practice area from team members in all areas of the firm, including tax, audit and risk assurance and advisory services, data and analytics, strategy and transformation, and AMF Media Group.

DOMINATING THE MIDWEST

As the nation settled into its "new normal" after 2020, Armanino's leadership team was eager to resume an inorganic growth initiative that had its beginnings in the middle of 2019. At the "Winning is Everything" business development best practices conference, I had a fateful conversation with Tony Caleca, the managing partner of a Top 100 firm named Brown Smith Wallace (BSW), about the future of our industry. Where other firms seemed fearful and resistant to the inevitable changes coming our way, Tony and I were so excited for the opportunities we saw ahead for our clients and our teams. Tony was also a board member of Moore North America and both of our firms were strong contributors to the Moore Global association, so I had enjoyed getting to know his firm over the years and admired their vision and execution in St. Louis, Missouri.

The more we talked, the more Tony and I thought our firms could learn from one another. A couple of months later, I flew to the Midwest and hosted a design thinking session for the BSW executive team, helping them to envision their future. That fall, Tony brought his leadership team to Armanino's headquarters and we all discussed what was working for our firms, where we struggled, and how we wanted to achieve our next stages of growth. The more the two teams talked, the more we realized it might be possible to achieve our future visions, going further and faster, if we took the journey together.

As I mentioned earlier, Armanino launched into 2020 ready to put all our organic and inorganic growth strategies into play. Joining BSW and Armanino together was at the heart of those plans and scheduled for the middle of that year. As the brutal economic impact of the pandemic became clear in March, Tony and I were having one of our weekly check-in calls. Almost at the same time, we said to one another, "We have to put pencils down on this combination." We knew we had to focus on our own people and our own clients and see this crisis through. Fortunately, both firms weathered the VUCA of 2020 very well and we were able to care for our clients, our people, and our communities when they needed us most.

"Because of the natural attachment our two firms had, at the point where we said we had to stop, BSW and Armanino actually came closer together," said Tony Caleca. "Our leaders started to reach out and work together on client challenges. It was a true, organic teaming that came about because of what we had learned through our merger discussions about our complementary strengths."

COVID-19 taught us, in general, that there were a lot of things we took for granted and that relationships really matter a lot. Our two firms working together during that difficult time created the foundation for us to move forward with the merger. Both organizations were better off, stronger, and better prepared to move forward than ever before.

We set June 8, 2021, for our announcement event in St. Louis. Because indoor event restrictions had been lifted in St. Louis and our teams had the opportunity to receive vaccinations, we invited the entire BSW team to a presentation at a local hotel. The first half of the presentation paid homage to BSW's proud fifty-year heritage in St. Louis. Before we share the rest of our story, I think it's important to take a step back in time and share the similarities between the founders of BSW and Armanino.

Harvey Wallace and Jeff Smith were senior accountants at Alexander Grant (which evolved into today's Grant Thornton firm). In 1971, they decided they had a better way to work with clients than their Big 8 employer, but they had no revenue stream. Jeff was selected to open an office in 1972. He found enough clients to make the venture worthwhile and in 1973, Harvey joined Jeff and they named the firm Smith and Wallace. They like to say they were just "two guys and a calculator."

Entrepreneurs much like my dad and Tom Jones, Harvey and Jeff slowly grew their client base. As a student at Washington University in St. Louis a few years earlier, Harvey had worked for David E. Brown, CPA. In 1975, David was in his late 50s and Harvey asked him if he'd like Smith and Wallace to serve as his succession plan. The day the two were scheduled to meet for lunch to discuss the idea, David was diagnosed with leukemia. He told Harvey he wanted to move quickly to protect his clients and his estate, so Jeff and Harvey rapidly transitioned his clients and just three months later, the firm became Brown, Smith and Wallace.

"David was with us for three years before he passed away. He was a good man, so we decided we'd always keep his name in our firm name," said Harvey Wallace.

"As we grew the firm, we were a little bit ahead of our time. We were really concerned about the people who joined our firm. We always wanted to make it a place where people would enjoy coming to work, where we would respect them as individuals and treat them the best we could," said Harvey.

Years passed and BSW grew from a small firm to a regional powerhouse. The Sarbanes-Oxley Act was a huge growth factor for their firm, like it had been for Armanino, and it brought the opportunity for BSW to deliver more complex consulting and accounting services to larger, public company clients. Fast forward to 2021 and BSW had two offices in the St. Louis region and 300 team members, with household name clients like Anheuser-Busch and Rawlings.

Returning to the day when we announced our firm combination, Tony did a great job sharing with the BSW family all the values and hard work that had brought their firm to this stage. He then told the audience that the best path to the growth they sought was for BSW to join Armanino. He paused for a moment to let the news sink in, then advanced to the next slide in his presentation. There, the BSW Mission and the Armanino Purpose were side by side. While they were written by different firms on different dates half a nation apart, the two statements read almost word for word the same.

"People were surprised, but I assured them that while our name was changing, BSW and Armanino had an almost mirrored vision and culture," said Tony Caleca. "What wasn't going to ever change was our deep care for one another and our highly personalized approach to our clients. Our focus throughout the entire merger process was on the opportunities this would create for our people and our clients. We wanted them to take advantage of the robust resources and depth of expertise that comes with being part of a Top 25 accounting and consulting organization with national reach. This was truly a partnership of opportunity."

I then joined Tony onstage and told the crowd that often we don't plan for the best things in life to happen. From a chance conversation Tony and I started in 2019, we had created this powerful union that was going to create amazing career opportunities for both our teams. I shared a snapshot of our firm's history, taking them back to our founders, who were also two guys and a calculator in their first year of business. I shared my dad and Tom Jones' deep commitment to their clients and their team. Emphasizing that the things that made our firm unique in the industry more than 50 years ago would carry us successfully into the future, I assured the team of our continuing commitment to do the right things for the right reasons.

I also shared that their local leaders would play an integral part in managing our national firm, with Tony taking the role of Midwest Market Leader, Partner Bryan Graiff joining our Board of Partners, and many others leading industry initiatives and committees across the firm. We thought so highly of BSW's program for female empowerment that we took their name and some of their key programs and renamed our Women's Advancement Network to "The Bridge." Finally, I shared with the audience that the combination of the two firms meant that Armanino would be a firm with $500 million in annual revenues in 2022. There were only seven other national firms in that revenue range and Armanino had the opportunity to stand out as unique, as the dominant firm in the Midwest, and as the employer of choice.

While I hope my words were inspiring to our newest group of employees, I believe the panel discussion that followed really helped elevate the level of excitement in the room. BSW partners Chris Menz, Kelly Weis and Ted Flom and Armanino Director Lisa Boyd and Partner Jeff Owens took the stage to share their perspectives. They all were so honest and open about how each of them had absorbed, and then embraced, the news of the merger and the audience hung on every word. But it was clear that the staff and managers in the room most clearly identified with Lisa. She had started her career at BSW and moved to Bolar Hirsch & Jennings (BH&J), before joining Armanino via merger in 2019.

"Two years ago, I learned that BH&J was merging with Armanino," Lisa told the team in St. Louis. "I immediately started asking the partners how this merger happened, and my staff came to me with a lot of questions. The partners didn't have all the answers I wanted, and I didn't have all the answers my staff wanted. But I think it was very good for me and for them to talk through the merger experience with each other."

Lisa then encouraged everyone in the room to go to their own partners and managers to ask all the questions they wanted. She told the group that all the qualities that had made BSW a great place to work were the same at Armanino.

"I know that Armanino's priority is for me and for all our people to succeed," said Lisa.

Tony echoed Lisa's sentiment in a call with our whole firm just weeks before the merger became official on August 1, 2021. He said, "I've been telling our St. Louis team that each one of you is going to leave a four-lane interstate and you're getting on an eight-lane interstate for your career. It's going to be wider and faster if you want it to be, and there is going to be a lane that fits you. That's the thing I couldn't be more excited about."

After the merger became official, Harvey Wallace shared with me that his greatest pride over his career had been watching the BSW family grow. "We created an organization that enabled hundreds of families to achieve their goals, whether it was buying their first home or sending their kids to college. We always tried to make sure that people had an opportunity to be successful and that's the reason we're all together now at Armanino," said Harvey.

EXTENDING OUR POSITIVE IMPACT ACROSS THE NATION

In July, Armanino achieved another huge milestone in the firm's history by firmly planting a flag in New York City and becoming a coast-to-coast national firm. Entertainment industry advisors Craig Manzino and Marc Rosen joined the firm as partners and brought their 26 professionals from Cameo Wealth & Creative Management into our business management practice. This new team added a comprehensive portfolio of arts and entertainment expertise, including Broadway and theatre, in addition to television, film, social media and music.

"Whether our clients are entrepreneurial entertainers, startups, enterprise-level companies or closely-held family businesses, we keep them at the center," said Marc Rosen. "That's what our team has always been about, and we knew joining Armanino was an excellent fit for us to continue our mission."

We quickly followed our New York launch with the opening of two new offices in key cities to support our nationwide expansion: Austin, Texas, and Chicago. These new locations consolidated existing teams who were on-the-ground in both Midwest cities and allowed us to enhance our service offerings for clients with business interests there. Geographic expansion is a key element of Armanino's strategic plan and a natural consequence of striving to better serve our national client base. We were excited to offer our growing team of professionals with new opportunities to connect at these local hubs and be better equipped to achieve more as a firm.

As we entered the last quarter of the year, Armanino made operational and expansion moves to continue to deliver on our Vision 2025 strategy. On a firmwide Quartercast call, I shared that over the past ten years, Armanino's revenue had grown nearly 450 percent, making us the fastest-growing firm in the Top 100 firms nationwide. Our strategic plan and revenue growth in 2021 had clearly set the stage for us to more than double our revenue growth by 2025. One thing we knew was that what got Armanino to our industry-leading position was not going to get us to our next growth stage.

Our leaders recognized that the world had changed drastically over the last year and a half and Armanino must continue its commitment to embracing change as an organization. Our firm's operational structure was strained by our rapid growth and organizational scale. That, in turn, was putting pressure on our people and our operational efficiency.

To address those constraints and position Armanino to scale for our next growth wave, the firm announced three new leadership positions and groups to become effective on January 1, 2022. Former AMF Media Group Partner Larry Hancock was tapped as Armanino's Chief Communications Officer to grow our internal communications department into a holistic strategic team. Tax Operations Partner Cody Page was named to lead the new Transformation & Practice Excellence group focused on improving the quality of day-to-day department operations. Finally, Tom Mescall's expertise was called upon to establish a new Chief Growth Officer role and coordinate our sales, marketing, and product development efforts. Cody was replaced by tax partner Eugenie Ooi and Consulting partner Ryan Prindiville took the leadership role for Consulting.

These three new departments set the stage for Armanino's future growth. But what did we learn about the future of work as we made our way through the COVID-19 pandemic? We became a better firm that is more flexible with a hybrid work environment. Yes, we know we lost out on the importance of human connection and relationship building within our business. Human interaction brings out the best of Armanino's culture and uniqueness. We are more than just a business, more than our profits. We have a deep care for our people and the community we've created, and the pandemic was the biggest shock ever to our community.

We don't have all the answers yet. We adapted in the moment, and we are continuing to adapt to bring back the health of our business. This is an opportunity to rethink how we work and get people to a point where they feel joy in their work again.

Armanino's leadership team introduced a concept that some have called

"Core Hours" to address the overwhelming number of videoconference meetings that took over our calendars as we worked from home. We will block a certain number of hours midday that can be utilized for internal meetings. Outside of those hours, we will not allow Armanino meetings. We feel this will allow our team to get more control of their lives.

In a big response to a real concern that many women have in the public accounting industry, we introduced a reduced-hour partner track. Available to all employees regardless of gender, we'll make it possible for all qualified team members to get to the highest level at our firm while managing the other responsibilities in their lives. Armanino will make sure that our people will have the structures and team support they need to be successful.

Finally, we announced to the marketplace that Armanino now has a four-year path to manager. We are committed to elevate people more quickly in this profession and we are rethinking everything we're doing as a firm to advance our team members. That means new approaches to hiring practices, to mentorship approaches and to professional development through our Elevate Learn platform.

We believe the ultimate area to innovate around is our people. The core of our business is people. In the early days of Andy's leadership, that meant the creation of the Armanino Leadership Conference, ArmaninoU and career pathing. Those were cutting-edge programs.

As we launched into 2022, we took another step forward to communicate who we are as a firm today and send a message to those we want to join us in the future. We announced the addition of another value to our Purpose, Values and Anchors. As my brother Andy so eloquently described earlier in this book, our PVAs explain why we exist, they define the soul of our firm, and they are enduring and foundational.

But after the challenges of 2020, the problems that remain with racial justice, and Armanino's increased focus on ESG and stakeholder capitalism, our IDEAL Team and leaders of the firm exhibited a willingness to be introspective about how we as a community can evolve and be better. What came shining through was our new Value: "Courageously Connected: We embrace a diverse connected community where all belong. Unmuted as their unique authentic self, everyone is valued and celebrated."

We stand as an inclusive environment where everyone belongs, where we are not blind to color, culture or lifestyle, but rather celebrate each person for the bringing their backgrounds and insights to the table. We believe this makes Armanino a stronger, smarter, and more resilient partner for our clients and our communities.

We are also rethinking the type of talent we have in our business. We're hiring industry-based experts, project managers, MBAs and strategists who will not only take our clients to the next level, but who will experience next-level growth at our firm.

"I think of Armanino being the standard bearer for innovation, and that all takes place in the context of entrepreneurialism," said Beth Kieffer Leonard, managing partner of Lurie. "The one thing about Armanino is that the firm is completely centered on their people. And that brings the most value to their clients."

One of the things I have always loved about our firm is our willingness and ability to change and take advantage of ways to improve in a world that is spinning very fast. These changes are one more example of our commitment to continuous improvement and not resting on our laurels. We will continue to embrace this approach as we move forward as a team. As I often say, I am more confident than ever that our best days as a Firm are ahead of us! In large part, that's because of our collective commitment to embracing new approaches and being the most innovative and entrepreneurial firm in our market.

STRENGTHENING OUR COVENANTAL RELATIONSHIPS

Just three years into my role as Armanino's CEO, one of my most heartfelt reflections is on how I have changed. Throughout my career up to this point, I was most passionate about building products and solutions for the marketplace, about creating growth and opportunity. I was entrepreneurial and externally focused.

As we teamed together through the changes that 2020 wrought, I felt a true responsibility for the 1,400 souls in this business. It was very personal – the fear of the COVID pandemic, the economic crisis, the racial injustice in our nation, the value of focusing on stakeholders over shareholders. I recognized the positive role that business could have in all of this. As a CEO, I had a platform to lead from the top. We could make changes to create a world that is a little fairer place.

What motivated me and our team was the renewed passion that we are servants to our clients and that's how we succeeded. It came across in a lot of my communications that we were able to do amazing things for our clients in a time of crisis because of the amazing people we have. We were better and we were stronger than we thought. I believe everyone at Armanino will look back on 2020 and say, "That was our finest moment."

I recognize now, our people are everything. The power of Armanino is our people. Armanino is not perfect for everyone. Our partner Dave Hirsch described us well when he said, "Armanino has energy and compassion all driving towards one result – the firm. We recognize that it's not all figured out, and we're still working on it, but Armanino has retained a sense of collaboration and family as a big firm."

The bottom line is that our core values take on universal meaning when they are reflected in how each of us behaves with our clients, with our communities and with one another. Armanino is the firm for those who want to be empowered, for those who want to make a positive impact. I remain humbled and so proud to be part of this team.

ARTES
CAPITAL

Artes Capital

Positive Impact on Our Clients

Armanino is always striving to improve on the philosophy laid out for us by my dad and Tom Jones. We continue to embrace our clients and help them reach their goals. Our business model is built on the bedrock of our founders' entrepreneurialism and reflective of the value-based relationships we seek with our clients.

For context, the accounting industry largely continues to embrace the "bill-by-the-hour" professional services model invented by Boston attorney Reginald Smith in 1919. One hundred years creates a lot of inertia, but Armanino has been on a journey to focus on the value we create for clients rather than the time we spend performing the work.

We began that journey by hiring Ron Baker as our Chief Value Officer. Ron wrote the pre-eminent book on the topic, *Implementing Value Pricing: A Radical Business Model for Professional Firms*. His role at Armanino was two-fold. First, Ron rolled up his sleeves and provided hands-on guidance for creating value-based pricing proposals for clients. Second, he teamed with Dean Quiambao to provide an in-depth value pricing academy for professionals across the firm.

We found quick success in going to market with key aspects of the value pricing model, including the provision of higher-value advisory services bundled with commoditized compliance services for a single price. We give our clients options to choose from and, as the name implies, our value priced proposals are based on the value our customers receive, not on the time spent delivering our services.

This entrepreneurial business model deepens our relationship with clients because we end up performing more services for them and introducing them to teams across more service lines compared to standard billable hour engagements. This, in turn, makes those client relationships stronger. Artes Capital is just one example from our hundreds of value priced engagements.

By exchanging best practices and new concepts at investment industry conferences, Armanino partners Jason Gilbert and Dean Quiambao had built a relationship of mutual respect with the founders of Artes Capital, CEO Scott Taylor, and CFO Brian Stocker. When they launched their new investment firm in 2020, Brian and Scott set out with a mission to be "artisans of real estate finance" and turned to Armanino to address their accounting needs. Jason and Dean provided a value pricing proposal with transparent billing for audit, tax, and consulting services.

"We chose to work with Armanino because their pricing allowed us to plan better, knowing what our true annual cost structure would be," said Scott. "The industry innovation that Armanino provides is a refreshing approach to what could be a dry and stale part of our business."

Brian added, "The key difference for me and Artes Capital is that we find we have a true business partner, a collaborator, another stakeholder, if you will, in our business. Armanino's approach has been to ask how they can better add value for the client. With other firms, it wasn't about adding value. It was about maximizing the amount they could bill for the bare minimum of work to get the job done.

"There's a long-term perspective on the part of Armanino and we share that," said Brian. "It's about recognizing that the economics will come if you build a long-lasting relationship. Armanino gets it. The partners come from the business owner's perspective, and they have the understanding, the professional empathy to give the advice and support that the client needs. It's not a one-size-fits-all approach with Armanino. We find it's really tailored to our needs."

Tiffany Allison

Courageously Connected

Tiffany Allison's greatest lesson at Kent State University had nothing to do with the C++ coding language her computer science professor taught. As he observed her classwork, this educator saw a spark in Tiffany. He wanted to empower her and scheduled a meeting for her with the Dean of Business. Their inspiring discussion ended with this advice for Tiffany, "You shouldn't be behind a computer screen. We think you need to be engaged with people, not just data.

Thankfully, that insight opened the path for Tiffany to find her way to Armanino, where she works remotely as a consulting senior manager from her Ohio home. Her light has shone brightly for all to see, and she enthusiastically engages with her co-workers and clients. During our 2020 virtual Holiday Party, Tiffany found a place in our collective hearts, singing a magnificent a cappella rendition of "O Holy Night" to the 1,100 team members on the call. And her insights into the systemic racism towards underrepresented minorities in the workplace opened up our firm's soul. Tiffany helped me and our leadership team to expand our understanding that the ultimate goal of diversity, equity and inclusion is "belonging."

"At every other place I worked, I was always the youngest person and I was always the only African American woman," said Tiffany. "Through the dozen years of my career before Armanino, there were only two times I was asked by a senior leader for my input. My vision of a 'Courageously Connected' workplace at Armanino began when I was scheduled to fly to our headquarters for a team meeting and became seriously ill. Scott Schimberg reached out to me, told me that my health was the most important thing, and rescheduled the meeting to a later date so I could attend and share my thoughts. I knew then that I wanted others to feel that they were important and seen and heard like I was in that moment."

Service is a big part of Tiffany's life. Throughout her career, she has volunteered with her church, the Delta Sigma Theta sorority, Youth Excellence Performing Arts Workshop and She Elevates. Tiffany even found time in her busy schedule to co-create "The Village" at Armanino, an informal hangout space for employees who are African American or of African descent to talk and celebrate together, where team members from the C-Suite to staff from all offices and remote locations are represented.

Tiffany was an early and avid supporter of the Armanino Foundation, so when the Board sought to add new perspectives through expansion, Tiffany was an obvious choice. Sharing her work and life experiences, Tiffany adds valuable insight to the the Board's guidance of our community service and grantmaking efforts.

After the murder of George Floyd, the Armanino Foundation and IDEAL Team sponsored a diverse group of team members to participate in a B Corporation Social Justice collaboration. Tiffany was a passionate participant who sought to share the lessons learned by the small group with the firm as a whole. In collaboration with the IDEAL Team, these leaders worked with the Operating Committee to define "Courageously Connected" and that has been Tiffany's proudest moment with our firm.

"When the new value was created, I felt like we were going to have progress," said Tiffany. "I just wept because I had been at companies where no one knew me or appreciated me and my thoughts. We may not always agree and that's okay. We don't always have to agree. But when we can share and have those difficult conversations because we're being our authentic selves, change happens then. Now, everyone matters. That's how we get to 'belonging.'

"I had wanted to be the first African American female partner at Armanino. Today, because of the opportunities I've had, my way of thinking has changed. Instead, I want to clear the path for anyone to get there and I will celebrate her just as if it were me."

empowerment - positive impact - community
5 years
armanino foundation

Armanino Foundation

Positive Impact on Our Communities

The Armanino Foundation's community service programming and grantmaking impact grew exponentially from 2019 to 2021.

In 2019, we introduced a new program called Dollars for Doers that provides nonprofits with grants of $10 per hour for time our team spends in volunteer service. Our team tallied 1,445 hours of community service across 25 different Dollars for Doers efforts. That was in addition to the 6,700 hours we logged across the country on our Great Give Day. Perhaps most exciting of all was the successful completion of our first international Volunteer Vacation – 53 team members, family and friends traveled to Chiang Mai, Thailand to teach English to elementary students and experience the culture and traditions there.

"Our team has an almost insatiable desire to give back and help those in need. I've received such heartfelt messages about how our grants and volunteer activities are so meaningful and inspiring to our team members," said Armanino Foundation Executive Director Mary Tressel. "We are always eager to empower them and create a positive ripple effect in the communities where we work and live."

To celebrate Armanino's 50 years in business, the Armanino Foundation coordinated a $50,000 Grants Giveaway. We crowdsourced the selection of the six grant recipients from our team members who cast more than 1,100 votes for 100 different charities.

"It says so much about your firm and your employees that you chose to celebrate your 50th anniversary by giving back to the community. This is so exciting – to make a difference in a child's life with music by providing scholarships to young musicians!" said Dr. Barry Knezek, executive director and co-founder of Lone Star Wind Orchestra and recipient of one of the 50th anniversary grants.

In 2020, the Armanino Foundation addressed the many pressing health and financial hardships caused by the COVID-19 pandemic by hosting major fundraisers for food banks, hospitals, and disaster recovery nonprofits. We also added Racial Justice and Sustainability as new areas of interest and increased the value of grants we made by 50 percent year over year. Working from home forced us to get creative for the Great Give. We offered 10 different "virtual volunteer" activities and our teammates were excited to work side by side with loved ones on the projects.

"As the spouse of a first responder, writing letters for Operation Gratitude during the Great Give tugged at my heart the most," said Lauren Nelson, senior consultant in Dallas.

"We are very moved by the generosity of the Armanino Foundation during this great time of need. Your support is helping us to open new 'pop-up' pantries and get more food to our community," said Diane Stark, manager of foundation partnerships at the San Francisco-Marin Food Bank.

At the outset of 2021, we launched a Financial Literacy program to provide budgeting and career courses taught by Armanino professionals to those in need. We were honored to be listed as one of the Top 100 Bay

Area Corporate Philanthropists by the San Francisco Business Times. And we wrapped up the year with our largest outpouring of volunteer hours ever at the Great Give at nonprofits across the nation, from New York to Los Angeles, Dallas to Denver, St. Louis to San Francisco and many more locations in between.

"Even our charity and commitment to the community is different," said tax partner Doug Sirotta. "Armanino is way ahead of other firms whose charitable giving is so corporate. We make our giving back so much more entrepreneurial by involving everyone at every level of the firm."

Beyond

Our History

The following chapters provide an in-depth look at our secret to success and the visions our future leaders hold for the firm we will become. We believe there's more for Armanino to do and we're not done yet. The voices you'll hear on the following pages chart an inspiring course forward.

05

Giving Our People a Voice

By Matt Armanino

> "I've never seen a firm listen to its staff more than we do. We change policy because of staff input. Our voices actually mean something here. We treat people honestly and realistically as our greater resource. I've never seen more wonderful, loving, smart people in one place. It's contagious."
>
> \- Ken Teasdale, Partner, Armanino

If someone asked me to boil this book down to one word, it would be *empowerment.*

Empowerment is at the heart of our purpose, values, and anchors. It is our not-so-secret sauce for the industry-leading growth trajectory we're on. Armanino's people have the confidence to challenge the status quo, to try alternative approaches, to create incremental innovation. Over and over, the team members interviewed for this book spoke of how they are supported here. This enfranchised approach to professional growth is a continuous feedback loop for the firm where each successful achievement sets the stage for the next achievement.

Armanino gets the energy of a startup by empowering our people. We are the best firm for those who want a platform to chase their own dreams, to build something. We're going to say "yes" more than "no." Your career is in your hands at Armanino.

If we rely on the leaders at the top to have all the great ideas, we're not going to get that far. Instead, we want everyone at the firm to answer the question: *What are your ideas for how we can make this place better?* When we're stoking that enthusiasm, it amplifies our collective energy and there is no limit to what we can achieve together.

This chapter is dedicated to the hundreds of people who have brought their passion to Armanino, revealed their ideas for how we could improve, and created the exceptional firm we have become. Paul Tarell, Lisa Boyd, and Kiyoshi William Smith are three of those team members who shared their voices with Armanino and made us better because of it. I've had the honor of getting to know all three on their journeys at Armanino and I'm proud to highlight their stories here.

Paul Tarell

Wickedly Smart

Paul Tarell started his accounting career at KPMG and told me that Armanino was the "exact opposite" of the Big 4 when he joined the firm in 2005. With my brother Andy, Paul started with the original Staff Advisory Board and, after being promoted, also served on the first Management Advisory Board. He left the firm and public accounting in 2010 to pursue a finance career in the technology industry and, today, Paul is President and CFO of Gaia, Inc., a $67 million global video streaming service.

"Armanino had a more entrepreneurial mindset and openness to thinking about the accounting industry differently," said Paul Tarell. "It didn't seem like you were going to get recognized for above average performance at KPMG.

"As Armanino grew, it became a really valuable piece to allow the earlier career folks to have some say through the Staff Advisory Board. It contributed directly to having that innovative mindset where you can have some impact on the overall direction of the firm. The Management Advisory Board was an extension of that ability. Not everything had to come from the partnership group – it allowed for more ownership and accountability for the firm."

"With Matt Perreault, I had the opportunity to help build the public company and technology audit practice at Armanino. I had the ability to build and develop staff instead of being dictated a 'one size fits all' approach to practice management from a central corporate office. At Armanino, it was pretty much an open book of being able to ask, 'How are we going to do this?' We really got back to the principles, understanding the client's business, and creating an audit program that added value for them. And we built up a team who had never worked on public company audits before - from two to 40 people in our San Jose, San Ramon, and San Francisco offices.

"What I've brought with me from Armanino to my career was that 100 percent personal accountability. I have always tried to embrace making things better as opposed to just doing the job for a paycheck. One of the reasons I could make the post-Armanino career trajectory so fast was the ability to take the knowledge I'd built by serving my clients at a high level and the growth I experienced internally at the firm. All that led to my new roles, and I instill that high level of personal accountability in my teams today.

"Today, my team is cross-functional. I manage the sales and growth and all the investor relations at Gaia. I benefitted from the opportunities I had at Armanino to establish the first Armanino University, the SuccessFactors employee review process, and the True Colors model for understanding ourselves and how we worked with others. Those experiences prepared me to manage teams that are not directly in my vertical of knowledge. That's all stuff you wouldn't get to do at the Big 4 and that exposure allowed me to feel comfortable getting into things in industry that I wouldn't have if I had just stuck to audit.

"The biggest lesson I took from Armanino was that everyone intended it to be fun to work there, but at the same time, they were very focused on the firm being a successful business. Being able to do both of those things translates into your life being a lot better and happier. I fundamentally align with the fundamentals and methodology that Andy and Matt instilled into the firm."

Paul Tarell,
Senior Manager at Armanino to President and CFO of Gaia, Inc.

Joined Armanino: 2005; Moved to industry: 2010

Lisa Boyd

Firm First

As we shared in Chapter 4, Lisa Boyd has the most unique career path of anyone at Armanino. She is the only team member who has worked at two of our legacy firms, starting her career at Brown Smith Wallace (BSW) in St. Louis and moving to Bolar Hirsch & Jennings (BH&J), before joining Armanino in 2019. Lisa has taken every opportunity to grow personally and professionally at each of these firms and, along the way, has empowered her staff and her fellow managers to do the same.

"I've only had 3 jobs since I graduated from college over 20 years ago," said Lisa. "I always wanted a workplace where I could stay for a long, long time. I started my career at Brown Smith Wallace, and I loved it there. Six years later, I was pregnant with my first child, and my husband and I moved back to Orange County to be near our families.

"When I got to California, I interviewed with a lot of firms, looking for a place that would check all the boxes that BSW had. I actually chose another firm initially, but the recruiter told me that Dave Hirsch, the partner at BH&J who I had interviewed with, wanted to talk with me to understand my hesitations. We ended up chatting that evening for more than an hour. Dave was very compassionate about the type of work I wanted and explained how I would grow professionally at BH&J. I was very surprised that he went that extra step. That call changed my mind. I always go back to it when I talk about what made me chose BH&J.

"As a working mom pregnant with my twins in 2013, I realized that a full schedule wasn't going to work for me to raise a family of three. Family always comes first, but work is very important to me, so I thought if I could reduce my schedule by 10%, I could have the flexibility I needed. I went to Dave, and he had no hesitation in helping make that happen.

"When we merged into Armanino, I wanted to see what was out there, what opportunities this bigger firm could offer for me to become more well-rounded. The IDEAL Team was really important to me. I always knew that being a Latina in accounting wasn't very common, but I didn't know there were ways for me to help change that. I'm coming into that now with Armanino. The firm is reaching out to find ways to broaden its scope and give everyone the opportunity to work here.

"I also joined the Management Advisory Board, and I gave a presentation during our pandemic 'Living in the Gray' session. I did that because I wanted people to know that they were not the only ones who had their lives turned upside down. I shared my story so people knew they could share the same thing.

"Then, I was selected for Armanino's Executive Access Program. All my firm involvement has greatly helped me to become a better person in the office and outside the office. I've become more outgoing and more of a self-advocate by joining these different groups.

"It was the culture that captured me at BSW, BH&J and Armanino. I didn't know exactly what the culture was going to be when I joined these three firms, but almost instantly at each one, I felt they were going to be good places for me. I want Armanino to continue to put its people first, which it does every day. I want that to continue to be the top priority as the years go on.

"Being part of a merger, coming into Armanino and seeing what the firm has to offer its people – it's been a really great experience. I've been learning and finding my way and it's just been the best ride so far. I'm looking forward to the rest of the ride."

Lisa Boyd,
Staff Accountant to Senior Manager to Tax Director

Joined Brown Smith Wallace – 2001;
Joined Bolar Hirsch & Jennings – 2008;
Merged into Armanino – 2019

Kiyoshi William Smith

Empowered

My brother Andy and I first met Kiyoshi William Smith when we had office hours at the former RBZ West Los Angeles office. Kiyoshi made it a point to knock on our doors and introduce himself with a handshake. He took the time to tell us about his professional journey, which started when his mom told him, "Everyone needs a good accountant."

Kiyoshi is such a well-rounded individual – outside work, he coaches youth basketball and promotes health and wellness by practicing mediation, writing poetry, and creating music. At Armanino, he has served as president of the first Toastmasters Club, chair of our Staff Advisory Board, inaugural member of the IDEAL Team, first Armanino member of the San Francisco National Association of Black Accountants Chapter, and member of the Armanino B Corporation Social Justice Task Force. Kiyoshi's very friendly, easy-going nature belies his drive to be a difference maker at Armanino and in the industry.

"I spent two years at KPMG and was on a committee, but it felt like the feedback we gave stopped before it went to the firm leaders," said Kiyoshi. "I wanted to go somewhere where my voice would be heard. If I have an opinion at Armanino, it truly does reach the top, our C-suite, and it sticks. It does not just get brushed off.

"I think it's very important to understand that it's all staff on the Staff Advisory Board, which means you don't have to wait to be a leader at Armanino. You do not have to wait on anyone to do that for you. I believe this is a place for leaders, a place where you can change the game.

"When I was invited to be a member of Armanino's IDEAL Team and saw the list of partners and other firm leaders there, I knew I wanted to be a leader in this effort. There was no hesitation – I needed to get on this team, I needed to make this commitment for the firm and for myself. I didn't want to wait to be a manager or a partner. I wanted to start now. I felt there was important work to be done.

"I am of mixed race. There's never been a time when I met someone outside my family who was Japanese, Polynesian, and Black. Being uncomfortable is kind of my comfortable. Being so different, there's no way someone can guess what I'm interested in, how I grew up, even where I'm from. That shows me there's this wide-open lane and it tells me things are going to be really interesting when my perspective continues to be heard more and more.

"There are very few black accountants in the industry. When you look at the leaders of any firm, they probably won't include someone who's black. We can combat that by having different routes of recruiting and we are now participating in a variety of ethnicity professional clubs and recruiting at Historically Black Colleges and Universities.

"We are having this conversation on diversity and inclusion even though it's 2020 because it's not something where there's a shortcut in your mind and you will know exactly how to create inclusion. Innovation has to do with thinking outside the norm. To be the most innovative firm, you need to be the most diverse and the most inclusive firm.

"At Armanino, I believe we are a community first and professionals second. We have room to improve everywhere, except our drive, our teamwork, and our positivity. This is perfectly fine because you can't really teach someone that drive and grind and hustle. It's great to know that we have those characteristics already.

"But we also continue to improve everywhere, whether it's how we communicate with our clients, or the industries we enter, or the diversity and inclusion efforts we're undertaking. It's part of our firm identity that we are always changing as the world is always changing. We are lifelong learners. I, too, as a Black American, continue to learn every day. The learning never stops."

Kiyoshi William Smith,
Senior Tax Accountant to Supervising Senior Tax Accountant

Joined Armanino: 2017

Our Best Days Are Ahead

By Matt Armanino

> The secret of change is to focus all of your energy, not on fighting the old, but on building the new."
>
> - Socrates, Philosopher

At Armanino, we have always held a tenacious belief that our best days are ahead. As Socrates advised in the quote above, our energy is focused on building the new. We'll continue to ask ourselves – just like our founders did – is there a better way to do things as it relates to talent, scope of opportunities, technology, and the business model itself? We will allow our people to make the most impact, to pursue their dreams with the fewest inhibitors.

Armanino will always be risktakers in the best interest of our clients, our people, and our communities. The firm has the financial bedrock and attention to key performance indicators that allows us to take advantage of market opportunities while not risking our prosperity as a business. Armanino's greatest attribute is the willingness to support those who ask the firm to be better and different. That will continue to make Armanino stand apart in the future.

"Armanino is at the top of the innovation scale for the industry – the way the firm thinks, the investments it makes in transformation, the way it deploys decisions," said Mike Platt. "Every other firm is at the bottom when it comes to innovation, empowerment, agility and rewards. I don't know any other firm in the accounting field that compares itself to Google."

Our vision is not to be the biggest firm. It's to be the best and most unique firm of the future. We owe our founders a debt of gratitude for our core: Armanino is an entrepreneurial business built on doing the right things for the right reasons.

"It's remarkable the impact Armanino has made on the accounting industry," said Tom Rosenbach, managing partner of Beene Gartner. "They're not really a CPA firm like all the other firms. They've surrounded CFOs with a suite of services and technology that even CFOs didn't know they needed until Armanino told them. No one else in the industry thinks of these things."

I could write pages upon pages of my vision and aspirations for Armanino in the years ahead. Instead, I wish to share a glimpse of our future in the words of just a few of our many up-and-coming leaders.

Bryan Graiff, Consulting Partner, St. Louis:

"My goal at Armanino is to utilize my corporate experience to add value. I'm on the Board of Partners and I'm working to develop the private equity industry initiative. I enjoy these entrepreneurial opportunities. I think Armanino is well positioned to be a destination for employees who want to be innovative and entrepreneurial. As a unique firm that attracts the best talent in the industry, we will be a North Star business partner for CFOs.

The firm must continue to push itself to stay committed to making the best decisions for our clients, our people, and our communities. Being unapologetic about growth is so important because it makes us a workplace destination – we will continue to be a great place to work and help our clients."

Ricardo Martinez, Audit Partner, San Francisco:

"When I came to Armanino in 2010, I had no idea how big it would be and how fast it would grow. Our organic growth and mergers and acquisitions have allowed me to thrive and take on new challenges that I would never have had at a bigger firm. I wouldn't have thought this when I first started, but in the future, Armanino will have a visible audit presence coast-to-coast. We will definitely be a billion-dollar firm and a Top 10 firm. The thing I like about Armanino is how we reward those who live the Purpose, Values and Anchors no matter how many years of experience they have. There are a lot of like-minded people here who will continue the strategy and maintain our PVAs.

I'm always curious about where the technology industry is going to go, what disruptive technology will pop up next. Because we've done a good job deep diving into the technology industry, we'll be ready, and we'll have people who have a passion for it."

Nghi Huynh, Tax Partner, San Jose:

"We're in the right industries at the right time. We're making the right investments in terms of technology and I'm proud of our firm for having the capital to do so. One area I don't want to see change is that entrepreneurial spirit we all have. People feel they can contribute to the overall firm and there's a direct impact. Our core values will stay the same. Those values have carried us through a tumultuous time. I don't see them changing because they are core values for a successful firm.

The future of Armanino is about creating a sustainable group with pride in what they are doing. The whole firm wants to succeed, and we have to remember that. We will be successful as a firm if we create a culture where everyone enjoys what they are doing. I have big aspirations for the firm."

Liam Collins, Risk Advisory & Assurance Services (RAAS) Partner, San Francisco:

"I was a partner at KPMG when I left to join Armanino. What really attracted me was the opportunity to build something from the ground up. I love the firm. My kids laugh at me sometimes because I get excited to go to work, but I like the people I work with. I care about them, and I want to spend my day with them.

The future for our firm is simple – nothing but growth! I am a big proponent of automation and changing the way we work to create industry-transformation technology. We're looking to a day when Armanino provides CFOs with real-time attestation reports they can review on their phones.

What's going to be a priority for the future is how we make sure we continue adding value to the community and do even more through the Armanino Foundation."

Kathy Ferguson, Audit Senior Manager, Dallas:

"With the pandemic, it has pushed Armanino into an even more relational basis with our clients. When the world gets shaken up, clients don't want a bot. They want a person, someone who can check in on them. I see Armanino's highly skilled people utilizing technology that allows them to spend more of their time on client connections and understanding their problems than checking boxes and doing procedures.

For women at Armanino, there is so much potential for growth. I'm excited where the future is going. I would like diversity and inclusion to not be a conversation anymore. The future of the firm is one where we are able to show there are equal opportunities for growth all the way through an individual's career. We embrace our purpose statement. I personally would never want our purpose statement changed – it is who we are."

Matt Chavez, Audit Partner, San Jose:
"It's important for Armanino to hold true to our values. Empowerment is the reason I'm here. We will empower more teaming and better focus on our industry initiatives as we continue to expand nationally. How can we differentiate ourselves? By staying true to what we're good at – our industry groups. It's what our clients want.

We'll be known nationally as a top technology firm. There's no limit to what we can do, so by 2030, we will add an extra comma in our revenue number to be a billion-dollar firm. The biggest difference between today and the future is that we'll be a nationally recognized firm, a big player across the industry."

Grant Lam, Audit Partner, San Francisco:
"I joined Armanino straight out of college at 21 years old. Over the past 18 years, I've seen us grow and grow. We'll see ourselves continue to grow in a smart and strategic way. I wouldn't be surprised if we were a Top 10 or a Top 8 firm. Our clients will be much more global in the future. We will be working with a lot of companies around the world and will have Armanino offices overseas. Maybe Armanino UK or Armanino China.

No matter how much we grow, I think we'll still stay rooted to the core purpose and values that our founders laid out for us. When I started, I felt like everyone cared about me and my growth. We will genuinely care about our people. We will look for ways to continue to do that."

Mary Tressel, ESG Services Practice Lead and Armanino Foundation Executive Director, San Ramon:
"Armanino will be the most philanthropic firm in the industry. Our team engagement in community service and grantmaking will be yet another reason we will be an employer of choice.

Our firm will leverage our experience as a Certified B Corporation to provide insights and confidence to our clients seeking to achieve ambitious environmental, social and governance goals. We will journey beside them to build resilient and sustainable organizations that have a positive impact on the future."

Larry Hancock, Partner and Chief Communications Officer, San Ramon:

"I'm proud that I'm working for the good guys. It's really wonderful when you can embrace your organization. I've always felt supported. We always try to get it right, and that applies to the IDEAL Team. We have a willingness to recognize that we don't have it right yet.

I really believe we can be a beacon to the industry. We can make a strong impact. We can define who we want to be. We approach diversity and inclusion with intention. Everything we want to change – we have intention behind it. We can achieve the magic of belonging. The value that brings to our firm and our clients is unbelievable. We will continue to trailblaze for our clients, our people and our communities.

Cody Page, Operations Partner, San Ramon:

"Armanino will always be the firm that says 'yes' to new opportunities, and that will continue to be our legacy. It's like working for a 2,000-person startup. A few years from now, I'll be saying that we're a 5,000-person startup…then, a 10,000-person startup."

Geoffrey Wayong, Data Analytics Director, Remote:

"I'm a data and analytics person, so the numbers tell the story. The future is going to be very bright because, so far, the track record is great. Every year, we crush the number. If you continue with the track record, the trend line is going to go up. Because Matt comes to the CEO role with a technology-centric background, he will continue to include technology in the firm's service lines and operations. That will continue to increase our value."

Ryan Prindiville, Consulting Partner, San Ramon:

"I had never really desired to work at an accounting firm. I looked at Armanino and I saw a sense of implicit trust here that I didn't see elsewhere. I also saw a firm with an amazing platform for growth. I've never been this excited about my career in 25-plus years. I hope we never lose our penchant for being entrepreneurial and introducing new service lines across our industries and geographies. My hope is that we can continue to leverage our purpose to be flexible and have creativity and ingenuity as we scale."

AN INVITATION

I'm so appreciative of the efforts of those who came before us – who cared about this business, who led this business. The roots of our past provide a direction for the future. This book fulfilled a desire that Andy and I had to honor our firm's history and to take pride in our founders, the original entrepreneurs, who opened so many doors for all the people who followed.

"I see Armanino as a firm that demonstrates entrepreneurship from their leaders and from the people they hire," said Rick Davis, managing partner of Elliot Davis. "Armanino's success draws upon people who are willing to come with new ideas, take risks, and then to go implement them into their vision for the future."

Armanino's success hasn't been an accident. Our future won't be accidental. We have more chapters to write, but Andy and I believe those chapters will sound a lot like what you've just read. Our firm's new chapters will tell great stories of smart strategies and creative things and new practices we'll build – the stuff we can't even dream of. But the enduring part of our story will be that our commitment to this culture will stay the same.

How will we keep our culture as we grow so quickly? It won't be our leadership team or our partners who make this happen alone. I believe in Andy's message to our team members and continue to share it at all our gatherings: "The key to Armanino staying unique and special as a big firm is each of you. As long as you care for the five people closest to you at the firm and help them to succeed, our culture will thrive."

The magic of Armanino has always been our people who care about their clients, care about each other, and care about the impact we're making together in our communities. I'm convinced we can win in the marketplace and make the world a better place at that same time.

And so, I invite you to feel empowered to share your thoughts with us. Whether you are an Armanino team member, or a competitor, a client, or a community member – you can help us to dream big and live out our Purpose: To be the most innovative and entrepreneurial firm that makes a positive impact on the lives of our clients, our people, and our communities.

Contact us at **TheFutureofArmanino@armaninollp.com.**

Afterword

By Andy Armanino

The Armanino story has always been pieced together from an exciting fabric of people and personalities and ideas and the hard work it took to accomplish them. My brother Matt and I are more confident than ever that the future for Armanino is bright because our team is writing new chapters of our story every day. We believe that the young people coming up in this business and those who will follow will share their voices and cultivate their own dreams into reality.

As we put the finishing touches on this book, I went back to the firm to relive one of my favorite activities. I sat in on an Armanino Staff Advisory Board meeting and asked the group to share their visions for the future. What could Armanino become? What might our industry and our clients look like in the future? I told them to imagine themselves with a magic wand and to dream big. I'm eager to share just a handful of the inspiring ideas that emerged.

"With artificial intelligence, we will be able to predict where and when climate-related disasters will occur and mobilize Moore Global people and resources in advance to support recovery efforts. We'll be able to build technology and equipment that can leverage the incredible wind power that results from hurricanes and put it into our power grids as natural energy sources for the greater good of the planet."

-Supervising Senior

"We'll create the Armanino Association of Young Professionals and make it available to college students and aspiring businesspeople outside the firm. We'll provide Armanino's best and only professional development courses and networking opportunities beyond our own doors and this will empower and incent others on their own career paths. When they discover how incredible we are, they will come join the Armanino team."

-Supervising Senior

"How are we going to make sure that a remote employee who has never stepped foot in an Armanino office will have the same connection to our culture as those team members who work in an office? Maybe we will use holograms, virtual reality, and the meta-universe to make this collaboration happen. We'll be able to put on a virtual reality headset and walk around any one of our physical offices to engage with our co-workers."

-Senior

"I picture Armanino made up of an incredibly diverse team and not just in terms of race. I see myself going to a college to speak in front of a huge audience and the science and engineering students will come to us to say, 'This firm is incredible and I want to be part of it.' Professionals are getting younger and younger, so I envision high school students interning with us, selected because of their incredible positive energy and potential."

-Supervising Senior

“We will empower more Moore Global firms to have their own Staff Advisory Boards. Armanino will become an advisory resource to helping other firms to create Staff Advisory Boards. Then, we will gather all the Staff Advisory Boards from the Moore firms together for a national conference and share initiatives.”

-Supervising Senior

“Artificial intelligence will get incorporated across the firm no matter what area of the business you work in. Armanino will be one of the only accounting firms that stops using billable hours throughout the firm through a combination of AI automation and human expertise to accomplish efficient and accurate professional services.”

-Supervising Senior

“I see us building a Craig’s List-type platform where our professionals can volunteer to support companies with a social or environmental impact organization that is trying to get off the ground. We’d have a 20-person team devoted to managing this Armanino Foundation pro bono platform and connecting our team’s expertise with worthy organizations year-round.”

-Senior

“When human beings start to develop civilization on Mars, Armanino will be there to help the new development become a more sustainable place both financially and environmentally.”

-Supervising Senior

2021 SAB Members who contributed to this future vision session included:

Bret Simmons, Brian Mullinax, Callie Baird, Cathy Nguyen, Chad Naro, Eric Chien, Greg Krussell, Hailey Bode, Jamissa Yasay, Jordyn Johnstone, Katelyn Price, Kiyoshi William Smith, Matthew Wallace, Michelle Gagnon, Monica Tran, Neely Koke, Richard (RJ) Coil, Seth Boschert, Taylor Douvikas, Tyler DeWitt, Yessica Gaytan

About
The Authors

Andrew J. Armanino

Andy's most gratifying activities today are giving back to the community through active involvement in the Armanino Foundation and inspiring young leaders of the accounting profession through the Moore Ambition program. He loves splitting time between Diablo and Tahoe with his wife Denise and kids Drew, Siena, Dominic, and Jaclyn. Andy also enjoys traveling internationally, fly fishing, golfing, and skiing.

Matthew J. Armanino

Beyond his passion for leading Armanino today, Matt's greatest pleasure comes from family time spent with his wife Alexa and sons Nick and Justin. He loves cooking, travel and meeting new people and his pastimes include hiking, fly fishing, skiing, and adventuring outdoors.

Mary E. Tressel

Mary also cherishes being with her family and is grateful for the inspiration she gets from her husband Mike and her kids William, Laura, Jacob, and Marco. She enjoys volunteering, reading, and exploring trails and neighborhoods in the U.S. and Italy.

Addendum

Firm Names:

Armanino & Jones, Accountants **1969**
Armanino, Jones & Lombardi **1976**
Armanino McKenna LLP **1998**
Armanino LLP **2014**

Business Combinations:

Ageno **1976**
Kimbell, McKenna & van Kaschnitz **1998**
Armstrong-Gilmour **2001**
Clare, Chapman, Storey & Bowen **2005**
ValueNomics Research Inc. **2005**
Thibault Associates **2005**
1 Source Solutions **2010**
FT Andrews **2011**
Factory IMS **2011**
Accesstek **2012**
Gateway Solutions **2012**
Rose Business Solutions **2014**
Berger Lewis **2015**
RBZ **2015**
LaRue, Corrigan, McCormick & Teasdale **2016**
Travis Wolff **2017**
Financial Strategies Consulting Group **2017**
Team Jenn **2017**
Barnett Cox & Associates **2017**
The Brenner Group **2017**
Bernstein Business Management **2017**
Fred J. Bastie & Associates **2019**
Bolar Hirsch & Jennings **2019**
The Resource Group **2019**
Niche Plus **2019**
Great Northern Advisory **2019**
Connext **2021**
Cameo Wealth & Creative Management Inc. **2021**
Brown Smith Wallace **2021**
Brigante, Cameron, Watters & Strong **2021**
Holtzman Partners **2022**

Geographic Expansion:

San Leandro **1969**
Alameda **1998**
Walnut Creek **1998**
San Ramon **2002**
San Jose **2005**
San Francisco **2005**
Portland **2010**
Naperville **2012**
San Diego **2014**
Los Angeles **2015**
Woodland Hills **2015**
Dallas **2017**
El Segundo **2017**
Downtown Los Angeles **2017**
Irvine **2019**
Seattle **2019**
Denver **2019**
Boise **2019**
Austin **2021**
Bellevue **2021**
Chicago **2021**
New York **2021**
St. Louis **2021**
Torrance **2021**

Awards:

Accounting Today Pacesetter – **2013**
Accounting Today Top 100 Firms – **2002-2022**
Accounting Today Top 100 VAR – **2010-2022**
Best Places to Work – **2012-2022**
Clearly Rated Diamond Award - Best of Accounting for Client

Satisfaction – **3-Time Winner**
Inside Public Accounting Best of the Best Firms – **19-Time Winner**
Inside Public Accounting Fastest-Growing Firms – **8-Time Winner**
Inside Public Accounting Pyramid Award – **2017**
The Firm of the Future – **2013**
Vault Top Ranked Firm – **2012-2022**
Vault Best Accounting Firms for Diversity Top 10 – **2022**
Association of Accounting Marketing Awards – **5-Time Winner**
Adaptive Insights Solution Provider of the Year - Americas – **4-Time Winner**
Inner Circle for Microsoft Business Applications – **9-Time Winner**
Sage Intacct VAR Partner of the Year – **8-Time Winner**
Telly Awards Winner – **2015, 2020**

Acronyms (in alphabetical order):

AI Lab Artificial Intelligence Lab
AMF Media Group Armanino McKenna Foster Media Group
ASK Armanino Services Knowledgebase
AUS Austin Office
BD Business Development
BEL Bellevue (Seattle) Office
BI Business Intelligence software
BIZMAN Business Management
BOI Boise Office
BOS Business Outsourcing Services
CHI Chicago Office
COE Center of Excellence
CORE Comprehensive Opportunity & Risk Evaluation
CRM Customer Relationship Management software
D&A Data & Analytics
D365 Microsoft Dynamics 365 Enterprise Resource Planning software
DAL Dallas Office
DEN Denver Office
DoBI Data Optimization & Business Insights
DTLA Downtown Los Angeles Office
ECG Emerging Growth Companies
ERP Enterprise Resource Planning software
ES El Segundo Office
ESG Environmental, Social & Governance Services
GP Microsoft Great Plains Enterprise Resource Planning software
GRC Governance, Risk & Compliance
HRBP Human Resources Business Partner
IC Internal Communications
IDEAL Inclusion of Diverse Employees and Leaders Team
IRV Irvine Office
L&D Learning and Development
LFS Law Firm Services
MAB Management Advisory Board
MDM Master Data Management
NAP Naperville Office
NFP Not-for-Profit
NYC New York Office
NOW National Tax Office (NOW represents the speed at which you get a response from Armanino experts)

PM	Project Management/ Project Manager
PMO	Project Management Office
RAAS	Risk Assurance & Advisory Services
RE	Real Estate
RPA	Robotic Process Automation (also known as "bots")
S&T	Strategy & Transformation
SAB	Staff Advisory Board
SEC	Securities & Exchange Commission (shorthand for public company clients)
SF	San Francisco Office
SJ	San Jose Office
SLO	San Luis Obispo Office
SMB	Small to Midsize Businesses
SME	Subject Matter Expert
SMPTO	Self-Managed PTO
SOC	Service Organization Control
SR	San Ramon Office
STL	St. Louis Office
TPE	Transformation and Performance Excellence
VAN	Vancouver Office
VBP	Value Based Pricing
WAN	Women's Advancement Network (now known as The Bridge)
WH	Woodland Hills Office
WLA	West Los Angeles Office

Works Cited

Journal of Accountancy, April 2002, "The Rise and Fall of Enron." https://www.journalofaccountancy.com/issues/2002/apr/theriseandfallofenron.html

Lorsch, Jay and Tierney, Thomas J. *Aligning the Stars: How to Succeed when Professionals Drive Results.* Harvard Business School Press, 2002.

Maister, David H. *True Professionalism.* Simon & Schuster, 1997.

History.com, October 11, 2019, "The Great Recession." https://www.history.com/topics/21st-century/recession

ConsciousCapitalism.org, 2021, "Conscious Capitalism Credo." https://www.consciouscapitalism.org/credo

Lencioni, Patrick. T*he Advantage: Why Organizational Health Trumps Everything Else in Business*. Jossey-Bass, 2012.

Christensen, Clayton M., *The Innovator's Dilemma: The Revolutionary Book that Will Change the Way You Do Business*. HarperBusiness, 2011.

Harvard Business Review, May 18, 2018, "The Five Behaviors of Leaders Who Embrace Change." https://hbr.org/2018/05/5-behaviors-of-leaders-who-embrace-change

Harvard Business Review, January 28, 2020, "Your Company's Next Leader on Climate Is…the CFO." https://hbr.org/2020/01/your-companys-next-

Cover Design:
Anne Marie Singer, Principal, Singer Design Studio

Book Design:
Jennifer Petersen, Creative Director, Armanino
Anne Marie Singer, Principal, Singer Design Studio

Made in the USA
Columbia, SC
31 May 2022

61171775R00096